"What makes David Woolverton's writing fantastic is that he is willing to delve deep into scripture and say what we already know but cannot hear due to culture's grip upon our attention. Engage this book and prepare for God's resurrection power to infuse you spiritually while he reassembles structurally what is broken and disconnected in your life and leadership."

—DAVE CORYELL,
author of *Less Like Hippos . . . More Like Honeybees*

"David Woolverton makes a clear biblical case that God does not buy into the American idea of ministry success measured by crowds but rather is invested in faith-filled remnants. This book will be of great encouragement especially to pastors of modest sized churches who are committed to the exhortation of 1 Corinthians 4:2 to 'be found faithful,' over and above any human measure of being 'fruitful.'"

—DAVID WOLF,
Lead Pastor, Grace Point Church, Newtown, Pennsylvania

"*Reviving the Remnant* is a powerful and timely call to weary pastors and lay leaders who still believe God can ignite revival through the faithful few. With biblical depth, personal vulnerability, and practical hope, David Woolverton reminds us that the Spirit often breathes fire into flickering embers—not celebrity stages. This book is a sacred spark for anyone daring to say 'yes' to God again."

—THOM S. RAINER,
Founder and CEO, Church Answers

"This book serves as a lifeline for every pastor who has ever felt the weight of isolation or wondered if their efforts are in vain. With wisdom, honesty, and practical application, David Woolverton reassures weary shepherds that God is still at work, that a faithful remnant exists within their congregation, and that God seeks the faithful rather than celebrities to lead them. This book will renew your confidence and restore your joy in the calling that God has given you."

—DAN GULNAC,
Pastor of Leadership Development, Ephrata Community Church, Ephrata, Pennsylvania

"Woolverton rightly pierces the heart with this admonition: 'Churches need to stop simply filling slots and start casting vision. People don't want to be cogs in a church machine—they want to be vital parts of something eternal.' His description of true revival sharply contrasts with the empty and unnourishing drink we've all taken at the well of celebrity churches and religious influencers. This book will bring a much-needed ecclesiastical sigh of relief. But it will also bring challenge that knocks the wind out of ego and influence."

—ALISA BAIR,
author of *A Table for Two*

"Filled with hope, Dr. Woolverton, shares heartfelt illustrations and encouraging principles of God's paradoxical Kingdom where the least accomplish great things and the languishing are made strong. Dive into *Reviving the Remnant* for a fresh perspective, vital guidance for daily centering in the presence of God, and practical wisdom for leading others towards the next Awakening!"

—JESSE GILL,
author of *Green Zone: Attachment and Flourishing for Christian Leaders*

"Woolverton gently reminds us, in whatever situation we find ourselves, that God is always with us and he can significantly use us in our weakness. Drawing upon biblical examples and church history, as well as from his own personal life experiences, he shows that we are not alone, that there has always been a faithful remnant that God uses to complete his working in this world. I highly recommend this book for everyone in ministry who is feeling overburdened by the good work they are doing and are headed for burnout. Woolverton shows us that as we are revived, we can once again thrive in our ministries."

—LARRY CALDWELL,
Chief Academic Officer, Kairos University

"*Reviving the Remnant* is a salve for the weary souls of those in the church who feel worn out, worried, or discouraged about the future of the Body of Christ. As you apply its practical lessons, you will no doubt see the Lord move in and among your own community of faith."

—JESS CAREY

Reviving the Remnant

Reviving the Remnant

Recovering God's Plan for Awakening His Church

DAVID E. WOOLVERTON

WIPF & STOCK · Eugene, Oregon

REVIVING THE REMNANT
Recovering God's Plan for Awakening His Church

Copyright © 2026 David E. Woolverton. All rights reserved. Except for brief quotations in critical publications or reviews, no part of this book may be reproduced in any manner without prior written permission from the publisher. Write: Permissions, Wipf and Stock Publishers, 199 W. 8th Ave., Suite 3, Eugene, OR 97401.

Wipf & Stock
An Imprint of Wipf and Stock Publishers
199 W. 8th Ave., Suite 3
Eugene, OR 97401

www.wipfandstock.com

PAPERBACK ISBN: 979-8-3852-6321-9
HARDCOVER ISBN: 979-8-3852-6322-6
EBOOK ISBN: 979-8-3852-6323-3

VERSION NUMBER 01/05/26

All Scripture quotations, unless otherwise indicated, are from The Holy Bible, New International Version®, NIV® copyright © 1973, 1978, 1984, 2011 by Biblica, Inc.® Used with permission. All rights reserved worldwide.

Scripture quotations marked (NLT) are taken from the Holy Bible, New Living Translation, Copyright © 1996, 2004, 2015 by Tyndale House Foundation. Used by permission of Tyndale House Publishers, Inc., Carol Stream, Illinois 60188. All rights reserved.

For Kristine
whose love, laughter, prayers, and faithfulness daily revive my soul.

Contents

Acknowledgments | ix

Introduction: When the Fire Flickers but Doesn't Go Out | xi

Chapter 1	The Remnant Pattern—From Exile to Awakening	1
Chapter 2	The Remnant Thread—God's Pattern of Renewal Through the Few	8
Chapter 3	When the Remnant Cries Out—Leading Through Weariness, Loss, and Lament	21
Chapter 4	When Ordinary Saints Show Up	31
Chapter 5	Spirit-Fueled—How the Remnant Carries Renewal Forward	46
Chapter 6	Multiplying from the Margins—How Remnant Renewal Always Reproduces	56
Chapter 7	Awakened to the Gospel—The Remnant Tells the Story with Passion	70
Chapter 8	Opposition and the Remnant Leader	82
Chapter 9	Awakening the Next-Generation Leader	92
Chapter 10	How Remnant Leaders Revive What Others Have Abandoned	108

Chapter 11   Staying Steady When No One's Clapping | 118

Epilogue: Reviving the Remnant | 131

Appendix: For Pastors—An Eight-Week Sermon Series Starter Outline | 135

Bibliography | 141

Acknowledgments

WRITING *REVIVING THE REMNANT* has been a sacred journey for me—one marked by prayer, reflection, and deep conviction. This book is not the product of one voice but of a chorus of encouragement, insight, and grace. I am profoundly aware of the many who gave of their time to bring it to life.

First, to Kristine, my beloved wife and prayer warrior—your daily intercession and unwavering belief in my call to "mentor and multiply" have sustained me more than words can express. You are my anchor, my partner, and my greatest gift. I love you more.

To my incredible network of friends and colleagues—thank you for reading early drafts, offering thoughtful feedback, and spurring me on every step of the way. Your support has been a steady wind at my back. I am forever grateful.

To the congregations I've had the privilege to pastor—thank you for entrusting me with your stories, your struggles, and your partnership on our mutual faith journeys. Your lives have left an indelible mark on my heart and have helped shape the very heartbeat of this book. The cry for revival is not abstract—it's born from the sacred ground we've walked together, the prayers we've lifted, and the hope we've carried. I am grateful beyond words for the honor of serving with you.

To Matt Wimer, managing editor at Wipf and Stock; Hannah Starr, my copyeditor; my typesetter; the creative mind behind my cover design; and the wonderful team of editors, marketers, directors, and assistants there—for the incredible partnership they offered me in publishing this book, my second with them. What a wonderful team of people. Once again, friends, your brilliant coaching, editorial insight, and commitment to excellence make me look better than I am.

Most importantly, to the Lord—thank you for trusting me with this message, for speaking through my weakness, and for stirring a fire in my heart for your church. May this book be a vessel you use to awaken, equip, and encourage those you are raising up. All glory belongs to you.

This book has been a labor of love, born out of a desire to see the remnant rise with clarity, courage, and conviction. If it speaks life into even one person, then it has done its job. Thank you for being part of that mission. I close with the prayer of the psalmist, which echoes the longing of every heart crying out to God for revival: "Will you not revive us again, that your people may rejoice in you?" (Ps 85:6).

Introduction

When the Fire Flickers but Doesn't Go Out

I've sat across from too many pastors and leaders lately who speak in the past tense—about their calling, their church, their hope. They're still showing up on Sundays, still preaching, still smiling for the newsletter photo. But something inside feels extinguished. The fire that once burned with clarity and urgency has been reduced to flickers. You might feel it too.

The thing is, I don't believe the flicker is failure. I believe it's proof you're still alive. In fact, I believe it's the beginning of something sacred, something "holy different." God doesn't need a bonfire and kumbaya singing to start a movement. He's always used the flickering embers of faithful, often forgotten people to light the way for others. And most times, those faithful few had no clue that God was about to use them to stir a revival.

For example, take Moses (Exod 3–4)—a fugitive in Midian, tending sheep in obscurity, yet God calls him through a burning bush to lead a nation to freedom. Or Hannah (1 Sam 1–2)—a weeping, barren woman whose faithful prayers in desperation result in the birth of Samuel, a prophet who would anoint kings, garner political and religious power and influence, and go on to shape Israel's future.

There's also Ruth (Ruth 1–4)—a Moabite widow, loyal and unseen by most, who becomes the great-grandmother of David and a part of Jesus' lineage; or Jeremiah (Jer 1, 38)—a young, reluctant prophet often ignored or imprisoned, yet used mightily to call the nation back to God in a time of decline. And what about Shadrach, Meshach, and Abednego (Dan 3)—all marginalized exiles who refused to bow to political pressure and who in the fire (literally) revealed the presence of God to an empire.

Take also Mary, the mother of Jesus (Luke 1–2)—a poor, young, unnoticed teenage girl in Nazareth entrusted with the literal embodiment of God's interventional strategy: Jesus. Then there's Anna, the prophetess in Luke's Gospel (Luke 2:36–38)—an elderly widow who worshiped in obscurity for decades only to become one of the first to have recognized the Messiah.

And what about the Samaritan woman (John 4)—a social outcast, morally broken, who becomes the first evangelist in her town after encountering Jesus. There's also Stephen (Acts 6–7)—a servant chosen to wait on tables, who becomes the first Christian martyr and catalyst for the spread of the gospel; and Ananias (Acts 9)—a seemingly unknown believer in Damascus who obeys God's call to pray for Saul, setting in motion the apostle Paul's entire ministry.

And those examples are just the beginning.

Historical examples from within our Christian tradition abound, as well.

Perpetua and Felicitas—young North African women, relatively unknown in their third-century world, yet their faith in the face of martyrdom galvanized the early church.[1]

Brother Lawrence—a humble monastery cook in the seventeenth century whose reflections on practicing the presence of God still shape spiritual formation today.[2]

And what about Susanna Wesley, John and Charles Wesley's mother? Raising children in obscurity, her devotion and spiritual discipline laid the foundation for a movement through her sons that would radically impact both England and America for generations to come.[3]

---

1. Heffernan, *Perpetua and Felicity*, 3–5.
2. Brother Lawrence, *Practice the Presence*, 15–18.
3. Dallimore, *Susannah Wesley*, 45–48.

INTRODUCTION

Then there's the Moravians in the eighteenth century—a small, obscure community whose 24-7 prayer movement and missions work helped lay the groundwork for the First Great Awakening.[4]

And who could forget people like Harriet Tubman, a formerly enslaved woman with deep Christian faith who led hundreds to freedom through the Underground Railroad, guided by dreams and prayer;[5] Corrie ten Boom—a watchmaker's daughter from the Netherlands whose quiet life turned into resistance, rescue, and redemptive witness after surviving a Nazi concentration camp;[6] and Jackie Pullinger—a young British missionary who, unknown and under-supported, moved to Hong Kong and catalyzed a ministry among addicts in the Walled City.[7]

There's also the incredible number of "ordinary" faithful church members, Sunday school teachers, elders, youth volunteers, and grandmothers whose unseen faithfulness shaped—and continues to shape—countless lives in faith and hope.

These are the real "remnant."

God often begins his greatest revivals not with the strong, the numerous, or the powerful—but with the remnants. The overlooked ones. The barely-holding-it-together crowd. The ones who know what it's like to lead through loss, conflict, transition, and spiritual fatigue and still show up anyway.

If that's you, this book is for you.

If you've ever stood at the edge of burnout and wondered if your best days were behind you . . .

If you've quietly questioned whether your prayers are still heard or your leadership still matters . .

If you've looked at a post-pandemic, post-Christian, post-everything world and wondered how the church could possibly find its footing again . . .

You're not alone. And you're not done.

4. Chilcote, *Recapturing the Wesleys' Vision,* 37–40.

5. Clinton, *Harriet Tubman,* 62–65.

6. Ten Boom, *Hiding Place,* 91–94.

7. Pullinger, *Chasing the Dragon,* 25–28.

INTRODUCTION

The remnant has always been God's reset strategy—not a leftover but a launching point—always working through faithful fews, tired prophets, honest pastors, unlikely leaders.

Well, what if the future of the church doesn't rest on grand strategies or celebrity voices but on the faithfulness of ordinary saints who dare to say *yes* again? Not a loud yes, perhaps. Not even a confident one necessarily. Just a yes rooted in surrender and fueled by a quiet trust that the Spirit is still at work. Still awakening. Still multiplying.

Let me be clear: I'm not writing this book because I have all the answers. I'm writing because I've been there. I've wrestled with grief, disappointment, conflict, and fatigue. I've watched as church systems strained and buckled under cultural pressure. I've buried dreams and walked through seasons of silence and spiritual drought. And still—I've witnessed flickers become a flame again—in me and in others.

This book isn't about chasing revival as a concept. It's about choosing revival as a posture. It's about praying, "Even here, even now, Lord, breathe on us again. Breathe on *me* again."

For those who are done with performance Christianity but not done with Jesus. For leaders and laypeople alike who are tired of chasing metrics but still ache to see lives transformed. For those who carry a quiet but tenacious longing for something more—a movement of the Spirit that isn't manufactured or marketed but unmistakably real. This book is for you.

What follows is not a how-to manual or a set of leadership hacks. It's a journey through Scripture, story, and soul—a trek into how God renews his church not just through mountaintop moments but through the daily *yes* of those willing to trust again. To hope again. To lead again.

We'll explore how God forms and uses remnants—people with nothing left to prove but everything left to give. We'll rediscover what it means to lead not from the platform but from the presence of Jesus. We'll look at the patterns of renewal that have draped God's plan from exile to Pentecost, from Ezekiel's dry bones to Anna's long obedience, from discouraged prophets to underground revival movements.

We'll hear stories of the burned-but-not-consumed believers who've dared to reimagine ministry when everyone else walked away. We'll meet people—ancient and modern—who said yes to God in the rubble. And we'll talk about what it means to mentor young prophets today, to cultivate resilience in the middle of grief, and to embrace Spirit-empowered discipleship in everyday life.

No, this isn't a leadership manual. It's a fire starter. It's a call to the ones still holding on—to believe again that God can awaken his church not through the machinery of modern religion but through the humble surrender of remnant hearts. It's for those who dare to believe that even now, the Spirit is stirring the embers again.

It's personal. It's real. And it's urgent.

Because the church doesn't need more polished performances. We need presence. We need power. We need renewal—not just in our churches but in ourselves.

So, if you're barely hanging on—or if you're hanging on by faith—then I invite you to read on.

God is not done with his church. And he's certainly not done with you.

Let's fan the ember. Let's awaken the fire.

Let's ask God to revive the remnant.

CHAPTER 1

The Remnant Pattern
From Exile to Awakening

SPIRITUAL RENEWAL RARELY, IF ever, begins with a crowd. It almost always begins with a remnant. And God has always had a thing for remnants.

Throughout Scripture and history, God has used a faithful few to ignite awakening in the many. Not the powerful but the surrendered. Not the visible but the rooted. These are the ones who respond in seasons of exile—whether literal, cultural, or spiritual—not with resignation but with repentance and resolve.

This pattern pulses through the biblical narrative. Exile, repentance, return, renewal—God awakens his people by working first through a remnant. While exile may seem like abandonment, in God's hands it becomes a crucible of transformation.

And the remnant becomes the kindling for revival.

THE EXILE WE DIDN'T EXPECT

Let's name what's true: in recent years, the church has been through an exile of sorts. We're leading in a moment shaped by cultural dislocation, social fragmentation, and spiritual deconstruction.

Church attendance patterns have shifted. Trust in leadership has eroded. Leaders are exhausted. Institutions are weakened. And so many people—good, faithful people—are asking, What just happened—and where do we go from here?

It feels like we've been scattered. Disoriented. Taken from what was familiar and placed in a foreign land of algorithms, division, polarization, and skepticism.

Welcome to Babylon.

Maybe not the literal Babylon of Daniel or Ezekiel, but the kind of cultural moment where faithfulness feels strange and conviction gets questioned. Where leaders wonder if anyone is still listening. Where hope feels costly.

This is where remnants begin.

ELIJAH'S CAVE AND THE WHISPER OF GOD

One of the clearest pictures of the remnant pattern is found in 1 Kgs 19. We know the story: The prophet Elijah, fresh from calling down fire on Mount Carmel, flees into the wilderness, exhausted and discouraged. Though God had just displayed his power, Elijah feels alone and abandoned. Even though he witnessed the amazing power of the Almighty, it all seemed to pale at the aggressive threats of an angry queen.

"I am the only one left," he told God. "And now they're trying to kill me too" (vv. 10, 14).

But God meets him—not in the wind, earthquake, or fire, but in a gentle whisper. In that whisper, Elijah hears the truth: he is not alone. God tells him that he has preserved a remnant—seven thousand in Israel who have not bowed to Baal (v. 18). God reminds Elijah that God has him where he needs him to be for a reason. A divine mission.

And that mission involves the remnant.

In God's economy, revival does not come from public spectacle, from top-down organizational strategizing, or from mega-sized infrastructures. Rather, it comes from the quiet faithfulness of those still listening to God's voice.

God always sees what we can't. He sees the others. He sees the seven thousand. He sees the next generation rising up. He sees the leaders in waiting. The mentors in motion. The hidden intercessors. The quiet resisters.

This moment is deeply formative for those remnant leaders. When the noise of failure or fear drowns out faith, the whisper of God reminds us: he's still moving. And he's never without a people.

"You stir us so that praising you may bring us joy," Augustine wrote in his *Confessions*, "because you have made us for yourself, and our heart is restless until it rests in you."[1]

You may feel alone. But you're not.

NEHEMIAH'S WALL AND THE POWER OF RETURN

Another pivotal moment in the remnant story comes in the return from Babylonian exile. In the book of Nehemiah, we find a cupbearer turned wall-builder, whose broken heart over the ruins of Jerusalem becomes the spark of renewal.

When Nehemiah heard that the walls were broken down, he wept. For many days, he "mourned and fasted and prayed before the God of heaven" (Neh 1:4). What an incredible thing for a leader to do—to grieve the brokenness that led to the current state of affairs for his people, and then to take personal responsibility for the sins that occurred well over a century before he was even born (Neh 1:6–7)! Nehemiah's heart broke over the exposure and vulnerability of his people in a land that he had only heard about in stories. His land.

Then after praying and fasting he moved. Into action. Taking risks unheard of in his day.

When he arrived in Jerusalem, he didn't call a press conference. He walked among the ruins at night. He inspected the damage. Then he rallied the remnant.

---

1. Augustine, *Confessions* 1.1 (Chadwick, 3).

"Come, let us rebuild the wall . . . and we will no longer be in disgrace" (Neh 2:17).

This is the remnant spirit: not nostalgia for what was, but faith to build what's next.

Notice that Nehemiah begins with prayer and fasting then moves with courage to rebuild. But the rebuilding isn't just architectural—it's spiritual. He calls the people to repentance, reforms injustice, and revives worship. Despite opposition from without and discouragement from within, the remnant perseveres.

Nehemiah's example teaches us that remnant renewal requires practical obedience. We pray, we repent, and then we build. God often uses ordinary people, burdened by holy grief, to initiate uncommon movements of restoration.

The pattern holds: exile—repentance—return—awakening.

THE REMNANT PATTERN IN SCRIPTURE

This rhythm of renewal is not limited to Elijah and Nehemiah. It appears across Scripture, forming a consistent thread of how God moves through history.

- Joseph is sold into slavery and imprisoned—but through his faithfulness, God saves a nation (Gen 45:7).

- Moses wanders in exile for forty years before becoming the deliverer of Israel (Exod 3).

- Esther risks everything as one faithful voice "for such a time as this" (Esth 4:14).

- Daniel and his friends remain faithful in Babylon, modeling spiritual resistance through prayer, courage, and loyalty to God (Dan 1–6).

- John the Baptist prepares the way for Jesus from the margins, not the center (Luke 3:1–6).

Each of these stories reveals a people refined by exile and positioned by God to catalyze awakening. Their power comes not from their strength but from their surrender.

From Genesis to Revelation, from prophets to apostles, God does not abandon his people—he refines them. He doesn't erase the story—he redeems it, writing it afresh through the faithful few. Through the ones who stay. The ones who return. The ones who lead others home.

THE REMNANT PATTERN IN THE EARLY CHURCH

Jesus himself gathers a remnant—a small group of unqualified, unlikely disciples—and entrusts them with a world-changing mission. After his resurrection, he doesn't appear to crowds but to followers behind locked doors (John 20:19). And in Acts, the church grows not by force but through Spirit-empowered witness, often under pressure and persecution.

The apostle Paul reinforces this pattern when he writes that "God chose the foolish things of the world to shame the wise . . . the weak . . . the lowly and despised" (1 Cor 1:27–28). God does not need a platform; he needs a people. He chooses the remnants—those still listening, still trusting, still faithful—to reawaken his church.

THE REMNANT IN YOU

Remnant identity isn't just a calling for biblical heroes or historical saints. It's an invitation for all who find themselves burdened by a lukewarm church or a broken world.

If you've ever grieved the gap between the way things are and the way they could be . . .

If you've ever cried out, "There has to be more than this . . ."

If you've ever stood in the ruins of disappointment, asking God to move again . . .

Then the remnant may already be stirring in you.

God is not looking for perfect people. He is calling the humble, the hungry, the hidden. In a world fixated on image, he's forming character. In an age of celebrity, he's raising up servants. He is gathering a remnant—not to preserve the past but to pioneer his future.

You don't need a platform to be faithful. You need a posture of surrender. When God stirs your heart, you don't need to wait for permission. You only need to listen—and respond.

Will you?

REFLECTION AND RENEWAL

Scriptures for Meditation

1 Kgs 19:9–18—God meets Elijah in the whisper.

Neh 1:1–11, 4:1–23—The remnant rebuilds under pressure.

Isa 10:20–22—A remnant shall return.

Rom 11:1–5—Paul affirms the remnant in his day.

1 Cor 1:26–31—God chooses the unlikely.

Rev 3:1–6—A few who have not soiled their garments.

Reflection Questions

1. Where in your life or leadership do you feel "in exile" right now?

2. Where do you see the remnant pattern in your own life or community? Have there been seasons of loss, pruning, or spiritual exile that God has used to deepen your roots?

3. What might God be whispering in this season? Like Elijah, have you been listening for God in the loud places but missing his voice in the quiet?

4. Can you name the remnant God may already be gathering around you—seen or unseen?
5. What does it look like to move from lament to action in your current context?

A PRAYER AS YOU BEGIN

Lord, awaken in me the courage of the remnant. Give me eyes to see beyond what's broken. Let me be among those who still return, still believe, still build—as a servant to the King of kings. In Jesus' name. Amen.

Chapter 2

The Remnant Thread
God's Pattern of Renewal Through the Few

When I first arrived at Saint Paul's Church in 2016, I knew that the congregation had been facing a decades-old conflict that had kept the two halves of the congregation at odds with each other. The primary issues revolved around what we used to call "worship wars"—the battle between traditional and contemporary worship styles. One of the ways the Saint Paul's congregation had "resolved" their dilemma was by separating the houses of worship into two different sanctuaries.

While I set to the task of getting to know the congregation—its values, its dreams, and its expectations—I began looking for an opportunity to build a new momentum while we were addressing the prevailing issues. It was in my third month that God created an open door.

In the rear of the contemporary sanctuary, consistently every week, was a row of five teenage boys. They were always very respectful, but they were teenagers hanging together in the way teenagers typically do in sanctuaries on Sunday mornings (if they show up at all).

Before the service was about to start, the Holy Spirit pressed on me an idea. I approached the boys in the row ahead of where they were seated. Kneeling on the seat of the chair and facing them I said, "Hey . . . have any of you guys ever heard the Bible story of King David's mighty men?"

They had not, so I continued to tell them the story paraphrased from 2 Sam 23:8–39. I said, "David didn't rise to leadership alone—he had a crew of warriors so bold they were called 'David's mighty men.' These guys weren't your average soldiers—they were fearless, loyal, and wild in battle. One took down eight hundred enemies with a spear in a single fight. Another kept swinging his sword so long his hand literally froze to it. One stood his ground in a field when everyone else ran. And three of them once broke through enemy lines just to get David a drink of water—just because he said he was thirsty! It was crazy! They weren't perfect, but their courage, loyalty, and grit helped build David's kingdom—and showed what it looks like when ordinary men step up with extraordinary faith."

I had their attention, but I could tell they were wondering why I was going on about this. So, I continued.

"I want to ask you guys to do something very important to me."

"What's that?" asked one of the boys.

"I want you five to become my mighty men. 'Pastor David's Mighty Men.'"

Intrigued, the same boy asked, "And what does that mean?"

"I'm not going to ask you to kill anyone, for sure. [Laughter.] But each Sunday, before this worship service starts, I wonder if you guys would join me in praying—together—for the service, for me, for God to do amazing things in our worship to touch people's lives. Would you be willing to be my 'mighty men'?"

"Wait," said another boy. "You want us to pray? *Out loud?*"

"Yes, out loud."

"I've never done that before. I don't know how to do that."

"I'll teach you. Would you be interested?" I was praying under my breath that they would say yes.

"I'm in!" said another boy. "Let's do it!"

"Okay. I'm in too."

Soon all five had agreed and immediately I had them stand, and together we walked to the front left side of the sanctuary, circled up, joined hands, and we prayed. The ones that felt comfortable praying out loud did; the two that had not done it before listened as I explained what we would do. It was a powerful five minutes of praying.

The following week, I sought them out, gathered them to our spot in the front left side of the sanctuary, and we prayed. Week after week this was our routine—praying for the service, them praying for me, us asking God to move in our worship.

About four months later, as I gathered my mighty men, a teenage girl was sitting with them. "Wait! What are you guys doing?" she asked.

Before I could respond, the one boy who had initially been reluctant to pray out loud said, "We're Pastor David's Mighty Men, and we're going up front to pray for him and the service. Come and join us!"

It didn't take long till my five mighty men became a cluster of nine teenagers who were praying at the beginning of the service.

And the adults in the congregation were watching. Both houses of worship were beginning to feel the ripple effects of a remnant of praying teenagers.

GOD RARELY BEGINS WITH A CROWD

When the light flickers and the faithful feel scattered, God doesn't panic. He doesn't shift into mass production mode. Instead, he reaches for a remnant—a thread of those who remain faithful when others fade, those who cling to hope when cynicism is easier, those who quietly believe that God's promises still stand even when the structure seems to crumble.

The story of Scripture is not the story of the powerful majority. It's the story of the few—the faithful, often forgotten—who become the catalysts for divine renewal. It's God's divine *interventional strategy* for humanity.

THE PATTERN BEGINS IN THE EARLY PAGES

When the world is swallowed in corruption in Gen 6, God doesn't raise up an army—he calls Noah, a single individual, to build an ark in the face of ridicule. Noah isn't famous or influential in his day; but he's faithful. He builds, he trusts, and God preserves a thread of life through his obedience.

Later, as Israel is born, we see Abram (later, Abraham), a nomad with no land, no children, and no status, being told, "Through you, all nations will be blessed" (Gen 12:3). He doesn't see the fulfillment in his lifetime, but he walks faithfully in a vision much bigger than himself.

This thread continues in the unlikely and the overlooked:

- Gideon, hiding in a winepress, is called a "mighty warrior" (Judg 6:12) and leads a dwindled-down army of three hundred against overwhelming odds.
- Hannah, weeping in a temple, gives birth to Samuel, the prophet who will anoint Israel's first kings.
- Ruth, a foreign widow, clings to her bitter mother-in-law and becomes part of the lineage of King David.
- The faithful remnant in exile—Daniel, Esther, Ezra, Nehemiah—preserve hope and identity while surrounded by empire and compromise.

Isaiah writes it plainly: "Unless the Lord Almighty had left us some survivors, we would have become like Sodom, we would have been like Gomorrah" (Isa 1:9).

God always leaves a thread. A remnant.

THE REMNANT AS A HOLY DISRUPTION

In the New Testament, the pattern sharpens. The incarnation itself is God's most radical act of using the obscure and ordinary to disrupt the status quo. And the story unfolds from there.

- Mary, young and most likely poor, is invited into the greatest miracle of all time: "You have found favor with God" (Luke 1:30). Not because of status or performance but because of availability—"I am the Lord's servant.... May your word to me be fulfilled" (Luke 1:38).
- Anna, the aging prophetess, who worships unseen for decades in the temple, recognizes the Messiah when others miss him (Luke 2:36–38).
- The Samaritan woman (John 4), shunned and scorned, becomes the spark for revival in her village.
- The early church, hiding in homes, persecuted, and scattered, carries resurrection hope to the corners of the empire.

Jesus didn't build around the temple elites or the Roman system. He built around fishermen, tax collectors, zealots, and women whose names history would've lost—except the Spirit made sure we would remember them.[1]

God, it seems, is in the business of disrupting our status quo, our typical ways of doing things. He consistently overturns human logic and presents an upside-down kingdom economy. The remnant is God's "holy disruption" in order to bring about his well-thought-out plan for redemption and reconciliation (2 Cor 5:17–19).

WHY GOD CHOOSES THE FEW

Throughout Scripture, God consistently works through the faithful few—not because he's limited by numbers but because he delights in hearts fully surrendered to him. When he chooses the remnant, it's never random. It's intentional. Here's why:

---

1. Matt 26:13, for example.

1. To Display His Glory, Not Ours

God often selects the least likely so that the results clearly point back to him. When the odds are stacked against the few and they still prevail, there's no question about who made it happen.

For example, take Gideon's army. In Judg 7, God reduces Gideon's army from thirty-two thousand to just three hundred men. Why? So Israel wouldn't boast, "My own hand has saved me" (Judg 7:2). God intentionally weakens the human side so his strength shines through.

The story of David and Goliath is another example. A teenage shepherd defeats a warrior giant not because of skill or armor but because "the battle is the Lord's" (1 Sam 17:47). The victory becomes a public witness of divine power.

2. To Cultivate Deep Dependence

When you're part of the few, there's no coasting. You're forced to lean in—to pray, to trust, to walk by faith and not by sight.

Elijah stood alone on Mount Carmel, confronting four hundred and fifty prophets of Baal. Before the fire fell, he had to rebuild the altar (1 Kgs 18:30)—a powerful picture of spiritual reformation beginning with the few (or even the one) who depend on God to show up.

Daniel along with Shadrach, Meshach, and Abednego refused to defile themselves in a foreign land (Dan 1:8). Their courage wasn't loud—but it was consistent. And their dependence led to divine favor and protection.

3. To Shape Servants, Not Superstars

The few are often formed in obscurity, not celebrity. God calls those who care more about his presence than platform.

Ruth, a Moabite widow with nothing to offer, commits herself to Naomi and to Israel's God. Her loyalty in the margins leads to her inclusion in the lineage of Jesus (Ruth 4:13–22, Matt 1:5).

Ananias—not the one from Acts 5 but the *other* Ananias in Acts 9—was an ordinary disciple whom God called to lay hands on Saul of Tarsus after his conversion. He obeyed, even though it was dangerous. His faithful, quiet obedience changed the trajectory of the apostle Paul's life.

4. To Mobilize the Marginalized

God often calls those overlooked by culture but seen by heaven. He elevates the voices no one else wants to hear—so they can become the very messengers of his truth and grace.

Look at Hagar. A mistreated servant, pregnant and abandoned, Hagar encounters the God who sees her (Gen 16:13). Her encounter with the divine in the wilderness reveals God's heart for the marginalized and misunderstood.

And there's the woman at the well—a Samaritan woman, shunned by her community, who becomes the first evangelist in her town (John 4). Jesus intentionally meets her where others would avoid her—and her story sparks awakening.

5. To Prove That Transformation Is Greater than Credentials

God doesn't need a resume—he needs a willing heart. The remnant is rarely composed of the religious elite. Instead, it's filled with the transformed—those whose lives have been gripped by grace and redirected by the Spirit.

Matthew the tax collector comes to mind here. Despised by his own people, Matthew is called by Jesus mid-shift at his tax booth (Matt 9:9). No seminary, no pedigree—just a simple "Follow me," and everything changes.

Even the Gerasene demoniac is part of the story. After being delivered by Jesus, this man begs to follow him, but Jesus sends him back home to tell others what God has done (Mark 5:19).

Imagine that—a man once tormented becomes a living testimony and evangelist in his region.

God's ways are not bound by time. The same divine logic that chose a shepherd over a king, a foreign widow over a princess, and a fisherman over a Pharisee still shapes his strategy today. The pattern of using the few, the forgotten, and the faithful has never gone out of style—it's embedded into the very fabric of how God renews his people.

When we trace the arc of redemptive history forward, we find that his preference for the remnant didn't end with Scripture. In every generation, God continues to call ordinary believers to extraordinary faithfulness—not through fame or force but through quiet obedience and holy disruption. These modern threads of renewal, though often overlooked, form a vibrant tapestry of God's ongoing work to awaken his church through unexpected vessels.

MODERN THREADS OF RENEWAL

While Scripture provides the theological foundation for how God uses the remnant, history provides the evidence. The Spirit's work didn't cease with the apostles—it's been moving like wind through the centuries, igniting unlikely fires in unexpected places. Time and again, renewal has risen not from the center of power but from the fringe—from the faithful few whose hearts burned with conviction while others slept.

These threads of renewal are not confined to one nation, denomination, or generation. They stretch across continents and cultures, revealing a divine consistency: God still awakens his people through the margins. Consider a few glimpses of how he's done so in recent centuries.

The Moravians: A Prayer Movement That Shaped the World

In 1727, a small group of religious refugees from Moravia (modern-day Czech Republic) gathered on the estate of Count Zinzendorf in Herrnhut, Germany. Though divided by theology and tension, a spiritual awakening broke out among them following a communion service. (If you're like me, I want a sample of the wine they used!) What followed was a prayer meeting that lasted—without stopping—for over a hundred years.[2]

Out of this humble community came one of the earliest and most influential missionary movements of the modern era. They didn't have financial backing, political support, or global networks—but they had fire in their hearts and knees worn from prayer. Their remnant faith sparked waves of global mission that would later inspire figures like John Wesley.

The Welsh Revival: When Worship Overflowed the Streets

In 1904, a twenty-five-year-old coal miner named Evan Roberts began praying for God to awaken Wales. He wasn't a theologian or a bishop. He simply asked God to "bend the church and save the world."[3] What followed was a sweeping revival that transformed a nation.

Over one hundred thousand people came to faith in a matter of months. Taverns closed. Crime rates dropped. Worship spilled out of churches into the coal mines and street corners.[4] There were no celebrity preachers or mass-marketing campaigns—just gatherings of humble, repentant believers longing for more of God.

The Jesus Movement: A Revival from the Edges

In the 1960s and 1970s, when American culture was unraveling in war, drugs, and social upheaval, another unlikely awakening began—this time among hippies and spiritual seekers on the West Coast. Branded as outcasts by the mainstream church, they were

---

2. Mandryk, *Operation World*, 363.

3. Liardon, *God's Generals*, 127. "Bend the church and save the world" is attributed to Evan Roberts, quoted in multiple revival accounts.

4. Evans, *Welsh Revival*, 23–24.

met by pastors like Chuck Smith and others who welcomed them in—barefoot and broken.

The Jesus Movement both surprised and defied the norms of traditional church. With acoustic guitars, open-air baptisms, and passionate evangelism, it helped launch Calvary Chapel and other contemporary ministries. Many of today's Christian leaders—like Greg Laurie—were shaped by its influence, even though it began outside the religious spotlight.[5]

The Hidden Church in China: Faith Under Fire

After the rise of Communism in China, many feared the underground church would disappear. Missionaries were expelled. Bibles were banned. Pastors were imprisoned. And yet—the church grew.

In the absence of buildings and official programs, believers gathered in homes, caves, and secret rooms. They discipled one another, baptized in rice paddies, and memorized Scripture by candlelight. I remember being humbled and enthralled by the many stories told to me by Dr. Samuel Moffett, my missions professor at Princeton Theological Seminary. Dr. Moffett served on the mission field in South Korea but communicated to us a deep passion for the church in all of Asia.

What the Spirit did in China in those years of exile and persecution was nothing short of miraculous. Estimates suggest that today, tens of millions follow Christ in China—largely because of the unwavering witness of a remnant willing to suffer for Jesus.[6]

The Asbury University Revival: A Student Movement

In early 2023, many of us saw the spark of awakening that ignited on the campus of Asbury University in Wilmore, Kentucky. What began as an ordinary chapel service turned into a multiweek, around-the-clock movement of worship, prayer, repentance, and

---

5. Eskridge, *God's Forever Family*, 5–7.
6. Hattaway, *Heavenly Man*, 132. Also see Aikman, *Jesus in Beijing*, 53–54.

spiritual renewal—without celebrity speakers, big names, or elaborate productions. Students lingered, wept, confessed, and sang, and thousands of visitors from around the world flocked to experience the palpable presence of God. I, along with many others, watched for hours online hoping to capture a spark of that presence.

The Asbury Revival was profoundly simple, yet it stirred hearts (including mine) with a deep hunger for holiness and marked a generation longing for authenticity and awakening. It served as a reminder that God still pours out his Spirit in unexpected places, through ordinary people, when his people are willing to wait on him.

Local Movements, Quiet Catalysts

Not every remnant movement makes history books though. Some never even make headlines. But their fruit remains a testimony to what only God can do.

- A pastor in a small Midwestern town who stays faithful year after year, preaching to thirty people with the same passion he'd have for three thousand.
- A retired woman in the South who starts a prayer group for her neighborhood that grows into a house church.
- A group of young adults gathering in a coffee shop every week to study the Bible and care for the homeless in their city.

These are modern remnant stories—often unseen by the world but deeply seen by God.

Each of these examples testifies to a truth our generation must reclaim: renewal rarely begins with the masses; it begins with the few. The remnant may be small in number, but they are massive in impact. They hold the ember of awakening that God breathes on in his perfect time.

The next generation doesn't need a celebrity-led revival. It needs a Spirit-led remnant. And the good news? That could be you.

YOU MAY BE THE THREAD

If you're reading this and feel unseen or weary, know this: you might be the thread God is using to hold the fabric of faith together in your family, your church, your town. Remnants don't always get applause—in fact, they rarely do—but they carry fire.

You may feel small. But remnants always matter to God. They're how he renews his people.

REFLECTION AND RENEWAL

Scriptures for Meditation

Isa 1:9—"Unless the Lord had left us a few survivors..."

1 Kgs 19:9–18—Elijah's despair and God's revelation of the seven thousand.

Luke 1:26–38—Mary's calling.

1 Cor 1:26–29—God chooses the lowly.

Reflection Questions

1. Where have you seen God work through "the few" instead of "the many" in your life or church?
2. Are you tempted to overlook the small, slow, or hidden places where God might be working?
3. Who are the forgotten faithful in your community? How can you encourage them?
4. Do you see yourself as part of God's remnant? Why or why not?

Practice This Week

- Write a note or message to someone who quietly carries the light of Christ. Let them know they're seen.
- Ask God, "Where have I underestimated your work because it looked too small?"

Chapter 3

When the Remnant Cries Out

Leading Through Weariness, Loss, and Lament

Every one of our churches is a church in transition. Every. One.

Large, small, old, new, traditional, contemporary, modern, post-modern. It doesn't matter.

Each church is either transitioning toward death (or worse, irrelevance), or it's transitioning toward growth within the mission that God has designed for it.

Now, you might say, "Well, our church is neither dying nor growing. Right now, it's in status quo, limbo. And it's been there for some time."

Status quo churches are dying churches. They are in survival mode—making or doing just enough to keep it in maintenance mode but not enough to engage the divine mission.

But it doesn't have to be that way. Each one of our churches is indeed a church in transition. Each church was planted with a purpose. And I believe that each church has everything that it needs right now to take the next steps in engaging the mission God has called it to live out.

Also . . .

Every pastor and every leader in every one of those churches is a pastor or leader in transition. Churches all over our respective neighborhoods are filled with pastors and leaders who are either transitioning toward "death" (or worse, irrelevance) or are transitioning toward growth within the mission that God has designed for them.

The good news is that because you're reading this book, because you're doing *something* out of a desire to make a difference for the gospel, the flicker of remnant hope is still burning in you. I believe that you are a pastor or leader that is transitioning toward new life in Christ, new opportunities for the gospel, and creating opportunities for your churches to discover or rediscover its call in the divine mission of God. In simple terms, you care about the gospel and the mission of God to make disciples for Jesus Christ.

But sometimes it's hard to see the hope through the hurt—especially when that hurt is chronic.

THE REMNANT IN ME

As I shared in chapter 2, when I arrived at Saint Paul's Church in 2016, we began addressing long-embedded conflicts that had divided the heart of what my district superintendent had called "a congregation of great potential." Over the first couple of years, God did amazing things to heal, restore, and rebuild. Growth began. Momentum and vision ensued.

Then the pandemic occurred. The fear that rocked our nation (and world) infiltrated our congregation. As with many churches, debates between the "masks" vs. "no masks" caused faithful believers to forget who we were—and we started reacting. Fear, anger, political conspiracy theories—it all challenged everything that God had birthed during the prior years.

After the dust settled and we regrouped ourselves around a plan, we discovered that a third of the congregation had decided not to return—either in person (preferring to watch online) or not at all.

And just as we were regrouping and rebuilding, the denomination I serve faced a seismic decision regarding human sexuality and inclusion, all within what had become not only a theological conundrum but also a politically charged nightmare that would lead to a denominational split. Even though the split was about so much more than issues of sexuality and inclusion, people focused on those catalytic debates foremost. More people left the church as a result. More tension and anxiety.

To be honest, already exhausted from the challenges of the pandemic, I was ready to pack it all in and retire early. For four straight years, I had been yelled at, accused of taking the wrong stance (by both sides), told I wasn't a good leader because I didn't come down stronger against "the other side," informed that longtime faithful members were now going to a different church because our stance on issues was too liberal or too conservative or too late or was not biblical enough or too biblically literal for them . . .

A classic no-win scenario. A Kobayashi Maru. Granted, the complainers were a clear minority. Most of the congregation rolled up their sleeves and processed through these issues like champions, even when they disagreed with one another. But that minority—their arrows and daggers were pointed and painful. And I stood amid the storm as a lightning rod. I was mediating conflicts left and right, trying to cast vision to keep the congregation moving toward something other than debate, trying to motivate staff, leaders, and parishioners to "remember who we are and why we're here," all while continuing to preach, teach, provide pastoral care, and bury the dead. Including my own mother who had developed cancer and passed away amid the chaos.

Often, I felt frustrated, angry, and alone. Like Elijah, at times I prayed for an exit. Retirement, for me, though, not death. Just saying.

Yet, in prayer, God kept reminding me that I was called to be his voice to the remnant. Those who remained. And to those whom God would yet bring under the ministry umbrella of that remnant.

Like Nehemiah, I was called to build—bridges of hope, walls of restoration, and resilient leaders within the remnant for what God was about to do.

God reminded me that my calling was not my own, but his. And he would sustain what he birthed in me.

You see, you can lead a revival and still feel burned out.

You can preach resurrection and still grieve a death.

You can love the church and still feel wounded by it.

Somewhere between the mountaintop of purpose and the valley of disappointment, many faithful leaders find themselves asking, What do I do if and when the fire goes out?

For the ones who didn't walk away but who now limp forward, keep reading. This chapter's for you—for those who kept showing up, even when the joy didn't.

It's for the remnant . . . who are tired.

ELIJAH REVISITED: THE PROPHET WHO WANTED TO QUIT

No story captures this tension more than the story of Elijah in 1 Kgs 19. Let's look at it again from a different angle. As mentioned in chapter 1, Elijah had just called down fire from heaven. He had exposed idolatry. He had confronted a king, a queen, hundreds of false prophets—and won! A revival seemed within reach.

But Jezebel's threat sends him fleeing. He runs into the wilderness, lies under a broom tree, and prays to die.

"I have had enough, Lord. Take my life" (v. 4).

It's a stunning moment—because this isn't a failure story. Elijah wasn't in sin. He wasn't compromised. He was just exhausted. Emotionally, physically, spiritually spent.

God's response is telling: He doesn't scold. He sends an angel. He gives food. He lets Elijah sleep. And then, he leads him to a quiet cave to encounter his whisper.

Elijah isn't replaced or rebuked. He's renewed. He's reminded about his role, his part in God's divine interventional plan.

This is how God treats weary leaders: not with shame but with sustenance and renewal.

JESUS: THE WEEPING SAVIOR

Look at another familiar story. In John 11, Jesus approaches the tomb of Lazarus and weeps. He knows resurrection is coming. He *is* the resurrection. But still, he lets the tears fall.

Why?

Because grief isn't weakness. It's love expressed in sorrow.

Jesus didn't avoid lament—he modeled it. He wept over Jerusalem. He cried out in Gethsemane. He questioned God on the cross.

You can be spiritually mature and still deeply human.

And you can lead others through their pain only when you've made space for your own.[7]

THREE INVITATIONS FOR THE WEARY

When the fire flickers or even appears to go out, we often feel ashamed, isolated, or tempted to hide our fatigue. But Scripture offers a different path—one that involves honest lament, restoration through presence, and rediscovery of purpose. These ancient texts guide us today out of the raw learnings of our forebearers. Their wisdom is a priceless treasure. Here are a few nuggets from that trove:

1. Lament Honestly

Biblical lament isn't complaining—it's faithful protest. Nearly 40 percent of the Psalms are lament. Leaders like Moses, Jeremiah, and David weren't afraid to say, "God, this hurts."

"Why, Lord, do you stand far off? Why do you hide yourself in times of trouble?" (Ps 10:1).

---

7. Woolverton, *Prophet and Loss*. This is a premise of the book.

I believe lament is actually a spiritual discipline. It makes space for raw honesty. It shows intense trust in God when we pour out our confusion, frustration, grief, anger, feelings of betrayal, and vulnerable doubt at the altar of our Creator. When we lament, it shows the depth of our faith and trust in the God who hears, the God who sees.

Lament reminds us that our pain doesn't disqualify us—it deepens us. By voicing our hard emotions before the Lord, we are choosing to believe (even if only by faith alone) that our "suffering produces perseverance; perseverance, character; and character, hope . . . [which] does not put us to shame, because God's love has been poured out into our hearts through the Holy Spirit, who has been given to us" (Rom 5:3–5).

As a spiritual discipline, lament connects us both to the grief work needed to move us through loss (anticipated, perceived, or actual) and on toward shalom (wholeness), as well as to a greater appreciation of our role in the mosaic of God's missional plan.[8]

2. Rest Without Guilt

Elijah slept. Jesus withdrew often. Sabbath wasn't a suggestion; it was a command.

You are not your productivity. You are not your church's attendance chart. You are beloved.

I have had to learn this lesson the hard way more times than I care to confess. With leaders, it's so easy for us to root our sense of identity, purpose, and "success" in the predetermined statistical outcomes and matrices of what we've been told qualify for "vital congregations." Well, quite frankly, in today's world, COVID-19—and its ramifications on church life—has been redefining what matrices are valid determiners of healthy congregations. The old paradigms no longer work. Yet, we continue to judge ourselves by the old standards—and classify ourselves as failures if we're not keeping pace with how things used to be.

---

8. Woolverton, *Prophet and Loss*. This also is a premise of the book.

It's exhausting, right?

Like Elijah, sometimes the most spiritual thing you can do is take a nap, cancel a meeting, or sit with silence and not fix anything. Because we just need our heavenly Lord to provide sustenance.

3. Let God Rekindle the Flame

Elijah didn't get a new calling. He was reminded of the one he already had.

God's words to him were simple and profound: "Go back the way you came" (1 Kgs 19:15).

The mission wasn't over—it was evolving. Elijah would anoint Elisha. He wouldn't carry it all alone anymore.

Sometimes when the fire feels like it's fading, it's not the end—it's the beginning of shared leadership and renewed community.

After my mom died, the weight of grief and years of accumulated chaos led me into a raw, honest conversation with God. I had been trying to hold everything together—systems, people, outcomes. After all, I had a doctorate in conflict leadership, and I wrote a book on how to lead through it. I thought I had the tools. I thought I *should* be able to navigate the terrain.

But I wasn't the only one weary. The congregation was tired. Our leaders were stretched thin. And in my effort to "fix" things, I had unintentionally taken on more than was mine to carry.

Through one of my closest friends, God reminded me of a truth I had taught countless times: in any family system, when one part over-functions, others under-function. Paul echoes this in 1 Cor 12—we are one body, many parts, and each must play its role. A simple truth I had forgotten.

The most faithful thing I could do wasn't to push harder—it was to step back a bit. To create space. To trust that God would stir others to rise. And he did.

God reminded me (again) that he called me to equip a *team*—to pour into them, to encourage them, to empower them. To create space for them, especially in a congregation where the default was to defer to the pastor. To give credit for success to them—and for me to absorb the hits when things went wrong. To allow them to exercise and execute the gifts that God had placed in their lives.

But here's the caution. When you've chronically over-functioned, stepping back—even faithfully—can trigger anxiety within the system. As you begin to empower others and shift the spotlight, expect resistance. Some may interpret your withdrawal as absence, neglect, or even indifference. Ironically, this discomfort is often a sign that you're on the right path. The system is reacting not to failure but to change. And change, even healthy change, disrupts the familiar—even when the familiar was unsustainable.

This reaction is known as a return to homeostasis: the system's attempt to restore its previous equilibrium, even if that equilibrium was dysfunctional. The pressure to resume your old role may be intense—not just from others but from within. You may find yourself second-guessing your leadership, feeling the urge to rescue, or tempted to sabotage the very progress you've initiated.

I've lived through that tension. I've felt the pull to step back in and "fix" things, even when I knew that wasn't faithful. But growth—real, communal, Spirit-led growth—requires trust, discomfort, and the courage to let others rise.

God doesn't just revive individuals—he revives remnants. And sometimes, he does it by reminding us that we were never meant to lead alone.

MODERN ECHOES OF RENEWAL AFTER BURNOUT

Yet, we're not alone in the challenges of burnout and lament. The embers of the remnant's fire aren't always visible during the times of our exhaustion. Others have walked this walk before us.

- Charles Spurgeon, often cited as the "Prince of Preachers," battled deep depression and physical illness.[9] Yet through his pain, his sermons rang with deeper compassion.

---

9. Drummond, *Spurgeon*, 11–13.

- Mother Teresa endured a decades-long "dark night of the soul."[10] Yet she served the poorest of the poor with unwavering devotion, her faith not driven by feeling but by resolve.
- Contemporary pastors and planters, some post-COVID, have rediscovered their calling not through strategy—but through surrender. Many have found healing by embracing smaller, slower, simpler rhythms of ministry.

The fire may flicker—but it doesn't necessarily mean it's gone.

In the next chapter, we'll explore how God often works through ordinary people—not just to revive the church but to lead it. Not with titles but with trust. Not with charisma but with character.

REFLECTION AND RENEWAL

Scriptures for Meditation

1 Kgs 19—Elijah's burnout and renewal.

John 11:32–36—Jesus weeps.

Ps 13—A model of lament.

Matt 11:28–30—"Come to me, all who are weary . . ."

Reflection Questions

1. Where in your life or ministry have you felt the fire dimming?
2. Have you allowed yourself permission to lament or rest—or do you tend to push through?
3. How might God be inviting you to encounter him in the whisper, not the whirlwind?
4. Are there people or practices you need to reengage to rekindle your calling?

---

10. Kolodiejchuk, *Mother Teresa*, xxiii–xxiv.

Practice This Week

- Set aside thirty minutes for intentional silence and reflection—no agenda, just presence.
- Write a lament psalm of your own—honest, raw, and sacred. Perhaps use Ps 13 as a template for your own.
- Reach out to a fellow leader or friend who might also be running on empty. Let them know they're not alone.

CHAPTER 4

When Ordinary Saints Show Up

IT WAS THE MID-1990S—GRUNGE and shoulder pads were still big, hair was even bigger, and overhead projectors were quickly becoming the height of worship technology. The staff team at my church at the time had sensed a growing hunger in the congregation to reach people through worship that spoke to a new generation.

Alongside our friends—Alisa, who played piano (and who was our church's director of worship), and her husband, Rob, on drums—my wife, Kristine, and I (both vocalists) prayed and dreamed about starting a contemporary worship service, one where people could connect with Jesus in fresh, Spirit-filled ways.

There was only one problem. We didn't have a band. At least not a full one.

But we prayed. And I mean really prayed—not just "God help us" prayers, but the kind where you're holding your breath and asking him to send people you may not have even met yet. Within a span of about four weeks, God did exactly that.

First came a visiting acoustic guitarist who happened to have been signed up to provide summer special music one Sunday morning. After hearing him share his musical skills, I said to him, "Might you be interested in a regular gig? We're forming a worship band, and we'd love to have you join us." After less than a week's time, he called me to say he was in.

Then a synth player with the coolest keyboard skills I'd ever seen joined in. He was a music teacher in one of the local schools and a friend of Alisa's. And he happened to have a friend who was an outstanding bass player. Both were in. Following them, an electric guitarist played his way into the band. And then, like something out of a jazz revival, a multi-instrumentalist walked in—saxophone, clarinet, flute, tin whistle—you name it, he could play it.

By the time we launched, the platform was full. Not just with instruments but with people who loved Jesus and believed in the mission.

That first service? It was electric. Not because of the music but because of the presence of God. Within months, it became the most attended service in the church. Not because we had cracked some code of church growth—but because the Spirit had breathed on something that began with prayer, faith, and the *yes* of everyday people.

What we experienced in those early days wasn't just the launch of a service—it was the quiet beginning of a movement. Not a flashy revival. Not a megachurch moment. But something deeper: the Spirit of God working through the *yes* of ordinary people. People with day jobs, families, and full calendars. People who weren't famous or platformed but who were available, faithful, and willing to grow together.

What we did not know until later was that a group of long-time church members had been praying for revival for over forty years prior—that God would use that congregation to reach more and more people for Jesus. They called themselves "The Ambassadors Class," and they were the powerhouse of faith that had led the children's ministries in their day, supported the pastors, visited the homebound, and passionately placed the heart of their faith family into the heart of their Savior.

Quietly, consistently, they had gathered in living rooms, classrooms, and pews asking God to awaken their church and ignite a movement that would reach their community for Jesus. They didn't need a spotlight—they just believed in the power of prayer and the promise of God's faithfulness.

Our worship team may have looked like the spark, but the faith of The Ambassadors Class contained the embers that had been glowing beneath the surface for decades, waiting for the wind of the Spirit to breathe it into life. And that congregation of three hundred once planted amid a plowed cornfield in the early 1960s became a congregation of over two thousand just forty years later—drawing more and more people into the embrace of a Savior.

This is how revival so often begins—not with celebrity but with surrender. Not with spectacle but with servanthood. The Spirit doesn't wait for perfect conditions or polished leaders. He ignites change through the gathered willingness of ordinary everyday saints.

THE CALLING OF THE ORDINARY

When Jesus launched his movement, he didn't go to the synagogue elite or the Roman establishment. He walked by the sea, looked into the eyes of fishermen, and said, "Follow me" (Mark 1:17).

Peter, Andrew, James, and John were working-class men. They had no formal training in Torah, no public platform, no theological degrees. What they had was the tools of their trade—tools that could be repurposed into a new mission. And they were willing. They said yes.

The early church was full of these kinds of people:

Lydia, a businesswoman and hospitable host, became the foundation of the Philippian church (Acts 16:13–15).

Phoebe, a deacon, carried Paul's letter to the Romans—arguably the most theologically rich document in the New Testament (Rom 16:1–2).

Epaphras, likely an ordinary local convert, helped birth the Colossian church (Col 4:12–13).

Tabitha (Dorcas), simply known for sewing clothes and doing good, was so loved her death prompted Peter's miraculous intervention (Acts 9:36–42).

Ordinary people. Eternal impact.

Somewhere along the way, however, we created a two-tiered vision of church:

> The pastors (or leaders) do the ministry.
> The members support it.

But Scripture says otherwise:

> To each one the manifestation of the Spirit is given for the common good. (1 Cor 12:7)

> You are a chosen people, a royal priesthood. (1 Pet 2:9)

There is no junior varsity in the kingdom of God. There are no spiritual spectators. Every believer is called, gifted, and sent. Renewal happens when the people in the pews realize they're also ministers. And they're vitally important in carrying out the mission Jesus inaugurated.

SAINTS IN DISGUISE: HIDDEN HEROES OF RENEWAL

Sometimes the most catalytic leaders are the ones history never records. Let's revisit a few examples—biblical, historical, and modern:

The servant girl in Naaman's house (2 Kgs 5) offers a quiet suggestion that leads to the healing of a powerful Syrian general—and a conversion to the God of Israel.

The boy with five loaves and two fishes (John 6) has no name, no sermon—but offers his lunch and becomes the vessel for a miracle.

Edward Kimball, the shoe-store evangelist who led D. L. Moody to Christ, never filled stadiums—but changed the world through one disciple.[1]

---

1. Wiersbe, *50 People*, 205–8.

Countless unknown house church leaders in China and Iran, who operate underground and disciple believers at great personal risk—no platform, just purpose.

And in your church? Maybe it's the quiet woman who prays faithfully each morning for those on the intercessory prayer list, or the retired guys who show up at the church wherever there's a broken pipe or a need to move tables, or the dad who coaches soccer and models grace for the middle school players, or the senior church member who brings donuts to the youth Sunday school class and listens deeply to the prayer requests they offer.

In my church they have names—Tom, Rick, Jen, Liz, Bev, Joe, Dave, John, Carol . . . and I could go on. God sees what most in the congregation and community don't.

Revival doesn't begin on a stage. It begins at the kitchen table. In the cubicle. On the bus. In the break room. At the playground.

MODERN THREADS OF RENEWAL

In fact, God isn't looking for more influencers. He's looking for image-bearers who say *yes*.

In almost every movement of God, it's the seemingly ordinary people who persist in prayer, obedience, and faith that shape the course of spiritual awakening. They rarely trend. They rarely tweet. But they embody what it means to be the remnant—those who remain rooted in hope and holiness, even when the spotlight shifts elsewhere.

Their stories echo across time and geography, weaving into a larger mosaic of spiritual awakening. And just as God used their quiet faithfulness in our church back in the nineties, he continues to raise up modern expressions of that same remnant DNA around the world.

Spiritual renewal is not a relic of history—it's a reality still unfolding in our time. In addition to the examples previously mentioned, consider these:

The Underground Church in Iran

In one of the most unlikely places, the fastest-growing evangelical movement in the world has emerged—not in megachurches or media campaigns but in the underground home churches of Iran. Led largely by women, this Spirit-led, disciple-making movement operates under threat of persecution yet continues to expand exponentially. Without buildings, budgets, or programs, they are quietly multiplying disciples through courageous faith, Scripture, and prayer.[2]

The East African Prayer Movement

Uganda and Kenya have seen remarkable movements of revival over the last several decades, sparked by deep repentance and prolonged intercession. Whole communities have been transformed, including corrupt institutions, as believers gathered for all-night prayer, fasting, and confession. Revival in these regions wasn't just a church phenomenon—it has touched education, politics, and family life. It was a holistic awakening, fueled by grassroots obedience.[3]

New Monastic and House Church Movements

In Western contexts—especially post-Christian urban centers—many believers have turned toward simple, incarnational expressions of church. The New Monasticism movement, led by voices like Shane Claiborne, sought to recover the rhythms of shared life, hospitality, justice, and contemplative prayer. House churches and missional communities have emerged in places like Portland, Brooklyn, and beyond—not in opposition to the church but as

---

2. Rosenberg, *Inside the Revival*. Rosenberg details multiple example stories.

3. Mulinde and Daniel, *Prayer Altars*. The authors give multiple examples throughout.

creative complements, reimagining what it means to live as the people of God in community.[4]

Campus and Gen Z Movements

Across college campuses, quiet spiritual stirrings are becoming more visible. Ministries like Chi Alpha, InterVarsity, and EveryCampus are seeing a renewed hunger for spiritual depth, especially post-pandemic. Students are forming prayer groups, worship nights, and discipleship circles in dorm rooms, study lounges, and even TikTok threads. Many Gen Z believers are less interested in church-as-production and more interested in church-as-presence—a longing that echoes the roots of every awakening movement.[5]

These threads may not always make headlines (though some have recently), but they mark something deeper: the slow Spirit-led renewal God often weaves through the margins. And while the stories vary, the pattern remains the same. God uses everyday saints—those unexpected ordinary people who are willing to trust, pray, and move forward in faith—to revive the church from the inside out.

THE MISSIONAL GENIUS OF THE MARGINS

God has always done his most lasting work through people the world easily overlooks. But this isn't a backup strategy. It's a design. Throughout Scripture, God chooses shepherds, tentmakers, midwives, and exiles—not just prophets and kings—to move his mission forward.

Moses was in the wilderness. Esther was an orphan in exile. Aquila and Priscilla were tradespeople who discipled Apollos. Lydia was a businesswoman who opened her home and became

---

4. Claiborne, *Irresistible Revolution*, for example.

5. Childress, "Engaging Relational Evangelism." This is one of the premises of the book.

a church planter in Philippi. These weren't anomalies—they were the movement.

The future of the church doesn't depend on a few stage-gifted leaders but on activating the faith of the many through the obedience of the remnant.

We've inherited a view of leadership shaped more by platforms than priesthood. But in Scripture, priesthood is not for the elite. It is the birthright of every believer. Peter's words still echo to the church today: "You are a chosen people, a royal priesthood . . . that you may declare the praises of him who called you out of darkness into his wonderful light" (1 Pet 2:9).

When the church awakens to the priesthood of all believers, the Spirit stops being bottlenecked at the top and begins flowing through the body.

EVERY SAINT ON MISSION

The early church exploded not because of megachurches or celebrity apostles but because ordinary people carried the extraordinary message of Jesus into every corner of life. Roman officials couldn't figure it out. How was this grassroots Jesus movement growing so fast? The answer: *everybody owned the mission, and they depended on the Spirit to make it come alive in them.*

As Michael Green notes in his book *Evangelism in the Early Church*, "The chief agents in the expansion of Christianity . . . were not those who made it a profession or a major part of their occupation, but men and women who carried on their livelihood in some purely secular manner and spoke of Christ to those they met in this natural fashion."[6]

We are living in a moment when the church must recover this dynamic. We don't need more church consumers. We need Spirit-empowered partners in mission.

So as leaders and faith communities, how do we create the kind of soil where that can happen? How do we cultivate churches

---

6. Green, *Evangelism in Early Church*, 173.

full of people who, like those musicians in my church in the 1990s, show up with whatever they have and trust God to do something beautiful with it?

HOW TO CULTIVATE A CHURCH OF EVERYDAY SAINTS

Revival doesn't begin in the spotlight. More often, it finds its way in through the cracks—through back doors, broom closets, after-school carpools, and hospital waiting rooms. It arrives not with fanfare but with a fire flickering in quiet hearts.

Revival begins with people who still believe God can do something with what's left—even if no one else sees it yet.

Revival has never been about the impressive but about the surrendered—a people formed by the Spirit, abandoned to the call, and sent into the world, not as professionals but as ordinary saints in the every day.

Why? Because revival is not an event—it's a people. A remnant. A surrendered handful of people who live like God meant every word he ever spoke.

So how do we cultivate churches that lean into that kind of faithful framework? I believe six postures lay the groundwork. These postures aren't formulas. They're invitations. And each one, taken seriously, can turn a community into the sacred ground essential for reviving the remnant.

1. Make Prayer the Culture, Not Just the Intro

Of all the practices that mark a remnant people, prayer is foundational. We could get everything else right—but without prayer, there's no fire in the furnace. Revival never comes without it. Not the "open the meeting with a word of prayer" kind but the kind that pours out hunger and hope before the God who still moves mountains. In Acts, prayer was not a preamble—it was the posture: "They all joined together *constantly* in prayer" (Acts 1:14;

emphasis mine). Before wind and fire came, there was emptying and seeking. Even Jesus began in solitude and struggle, not in strategy (Luke 4:1–2).

Remnant communities don't just pray out of duty—they pray because they're desperate. Desperate for God's presence. Desperate for God's mercy. Desperate for more than they could ever produce on their own. They're done with performance and programs alone. They want Holy Spirit power. And they know it won't come unless they kneel first.

This kind of prayer becomes the culture, not the garnish. It seeps into worship, into meetings, into the homes of the people. It's modeled by leaders, shared in circles, groaned in secret. When churches cultivate expectancy through prayer, the atmosphere changes. And that's when the Spirit moves—not always loudly but always deeply.

2. Place Calling over Celebrity

In a culture that prizes charisma, churches can fall into the trap of mistaking stage presence for spiritual authority. But God doesn't call the spotlighted—he calls the surrendered. Paul's reminder to the Corinthians still stands: "Not many of you were wise . . . not many were influential" (1 Cor 1:26)—but that didn't disqualify them. It prepared them.

We live in a world that rewards the loudest voice, the most curated presence, the highest view count, the greatest number of likes. But the kingdom has always moved through the lowly and overlooked. Jesus could've come through Rome, center stage. Instead, he entered through a peasant girl's womb in a forgotten corner of Israel (Luke 1:48). He never called influencers—he called fishermen, tax collectors, zealots, and sinners. In fact, his ministry started not on a stage but in a backwater town (John 1:46).

Paul reminds us in 2 Tim 1:9 that we are saved and "called with *a holy calling*, not because of our works but *because of his own purpose and grace*" (emphasis mine). This isn't about anti-excellence;

it's about rooting excellence in humility, not hype. In God's economy, obscurity is not disqualification—it's often preparation.

Remnant-minded churches refuse to idolize giftedness. Instead, they look for faithfulness in the shadows. They call out purpose in the overlooked. Because in God's economy, the one folding bulletins might be the one carrying revival in their prayers. Every greeter, every behind-the-scenes intercessor, every youth mentor or nursery volunteer is already a vital thread in the tapestry God is weaving. We just need eyes to see them.

3. Normalize Participation over Performance

Church isn't meant to be watched—it's meant to be lived. But for many, church has become a stage show: a few perform, the rest spectate. Especially in our post-COVID world where it's now easier for us to "do church" from the comforts of our home while wearing our pajamas and eating our Corn Flakes and Pop-Tarts. While contextually understandable, that has never been the New Testament vision.

When the early church gathered, "every one of you" brought something (1 Cor 14:26). Today, the Spirit still wants to speak—not just through pastors but through testimonies, prayers, questions, and holy moments sparked by everyday people. That means creating space for participation that isn't perfect but real, authentic, raw. For children to pray on the platform. For newcomers to share their story. For risk-taking discipleship to be a norm, not an exception.

Over the decades, to get volunteers many of our churches have dumbed down the responsibilities we place on people. We've made it a plug-and-play ministry environment where the teachers in our kid's ministry classes, for example, just need to show up and read a script. To get more people in the pews, many of us have minimized expectations for membership—even while sports teams are increasing their demands on families, crowding out worship on weekends. We are now reaping what we, as a society, have sown.

Participation is messy, but it's also where the fire is. People grow when they're trusted to try, not just expected to watch, when they're given vital ministries and asked to commit to investing in the lives of others with the most life-changing message of the gospel.

4. Form Habits of Presence, Not Just Programs of Activity

Remnant people aren't defined by how many church things they do. They're rooted in who they're becoming. They've learned to live with Jesus in the quiet spaces—the early morning commute, the moment between meetings, the kitchen sink prayers.

Too often, we mistake spiritual busyness for spiritual depth. But God revives a people through rhythms, not rush. Through margin, not just movement.

Remnant communities form people in habits of presence: learning to listen to God in silence, fasting from the habits and activities that keep us anchored to our brokenness, reading Scripture slowly and communally, walking in daily repentance and Spirit-led awareness. These aren't extra activities. They're the trellis on which revival grows.

Remnant people aren't just active in ministry—they're anchored in Jesus. Their life with God isn't outsourced to Sunday mornings. In fact, many revivals in history have been sparked not through strategic initiatives but through simple, faithful rhythms of prayer, repentance, and the word.

A church of everyday saints helps people *be with* Jesus before *doing for* Jesus. It teaches people how to listen to the Spirit, read Scripture devotionally and communally, and grow in obedience. Spiritual formation isn't optional. It's the root system of revival.

Emerging generations are craving the things of God. And God has been inviting each generation into intimacy with himself. How are we equipping our people in discovering that intimacy?

5. Celebrate Faithfulness over Flash

In a world where viral often trumps valuable, it's easy to believe that fruitfulness comes with fireworks. But the kingdom moves at a different pace.

The heroes of Heb 11 aren't success stories—they're endurance stories. People who trusted God in famine, obscurity, exile, persecution. People who waited a lifetime and still "welcomed the promise from afar" (v. 13). Revival doesn't ride in on bright lights—it lingers around long obedience, over humble repentance.

Think of Anna. She prayed and fasted in the temple for decades. No spotlight, no applause. But she recognized the Messiah when he was still a baby in the arms of his mother (Luke 2:36–38). That's the fruit of long obedience.

Remnant churches learn to look for the quiet heroes. The person who's discipled teens for fifteen years. The one who opens the doors before anyone arrives. The leader who's kept showing up even after the enthusiasm faded. When we honor the faithful, we redefine what success looks like—and we build a culture where roots matter, giving us the stability to reach out and bear more fruit for the kingdom.

6. Invite People into a Bigger Story

As prayer fuels the fire, mission gives it direction. The remnant doesn't just pray for themselves—they pray to be sent. That's why the next move of God won't come through a cadre of gifted or charismatic leaders but through everyday saints who see their ordinary lives as sacred callings, part of a larger mission.

To get there, churches need to stop simply filling slots and start casting vision. People don't want to be cogs in a church machine—they want to be vital parts of something eternal. So, we need to speak life into their roles. We need to remind them that the way they serve—the way they pray, parent, teach, greet, mentor, advocate, show up—matters profoundly in the kingdom.

The earliest believers were everyday people—ordinary men, women, children, the poor, the well-off, the marginalized, the overlooked, the previously scrupulous, those longing for a hope that they could not find on their own terms—forever changed by a man, a cross, and an empty tomb. And they turned the world upside down because they believed Jesus had sent them on mission (Acts 1:8). A church of everyday saints invites people into God's mosaic masterpiece—and then equips them to go.

Everyone has a vital part in that masterpiece. It's not about the size of the role; it's about the surrender behind it. When people realize that their quiet faithfulness is actually how God renews the world, they step in with joy. They give not out of guilt but out of calling. They serve not to survive a Sunday schedule but because they've caught a glimpse of the story they're part of.

In chapter 5, we'll go deeper with how the Spirit breathes life into this kind of remnant people—not just to sustain them but to multiply them. Because Spirit-filled saints don't just gather—they go.

REFLECTION AND RENEWAL

Scriptures for Meditation

1 Cor 1:26-29—"God chose the lowly things of this world . . ."

Acts 4:13—"They were unschooled, ordinary men . . . and they took note that these men had been with Jesus."

Luke 2:36-38—Anna's years of faithfulness and reward.

Rom 12:1—Offering our lives as "living sacrifices."

Col 3:16-17—Letting the word dwell richly among the community.

Reflection Questions

1. Have you ever disqualified yourself from ministry because you didn't feel "official" enough?
2. Who are the ordinary saints in your life who have impacted you deeply?
3. In what ways has your church elevated platformed personalities over called people? What needs to shift?
4. Where are you currently cultivating faithful participation and expectancy in your congregation—and where is there room to grow?
5. Which of the six practices mentioned in this chapter do you most need to implement in your church or life?

Practice This Week

- Encourage someone who's not on staff but is living faithfully. Speak blessing into their "ordinary" role.
- Reassess your own gifts and ask, Where am I underestimating my kingdom impact?
- Begin a "Hidden Saints" journal: write down the unseen acts of love, service, or sacrifice you witness each week. Pray for those individuals.

CHAPTER 5

Spirit-Fueled

How the Remnant Carries Renewal Forward

I ONCE STOOD AT the edge of burnout with a calendar full of meetings and a heart running on fumes. I had navigated the pandemic and way too quickly jumped headlong into the chaos of our denominational conflict—all while navigating the practical and emotional challenges of my mom's cancer diagnosis, treatments, and ultimate death. Ministry was still moving, and I was doing a fine job functioning within my professional roles, but something emotionally inside me had stalled. We had programs, plans, and polished presentations—but I kept wondering if any of it was really moving the needle for the kingdom of God.

It was during one of those foggy seasons when a member of our church—quiet, unnoticed, and faithful—walked up to me after a service. "Pastor," she said, "I've been praying for you every day for the past year. I just wanted you to know you're not alone."

That sentence undid me.

She had no title. She wasn't on a board or a platform. But she had authority with God. She was what I now know to be a remnant leader—one of those rare saints whose impact runs deeper than applause and longer than trends. She wasn't flashy, but she was faithful. And God was using her to hold the line and keep the flame lit when, emotionally, I couldn't see the way forward.

That moment became a turning point for me—not because a strategic breakthrough had occurred but because I realized what kind of leader I wanted to become. Not just a visionary, or a communicator, or even a strategic thinker—but someone whose quiet consistency was used by God to stir revival in unseen places.

In this chapter, we'll explore the traits that define leaders like that. Not the headline-makers but the heart-steadying, Spirit-led, resurrection-trusting leaders God uses to revive the church from the inside out.

TRAITS OF REMNANT LEADERS

If God's plan to awaken the church involves using ordinary saints in extraordinary ways, then it's vital to understand the kind of character God cultivates in those he chooses. These aren't self-appointed heroes. They're often reluctant, hidden, or even broken leaders who allow the Spirit to do something sacred in them before doing something visible through them.

Remnant leaders don't fit into a cookie-cutter mold. But they often share a recognizable pattern of character and conviction—a spiritual DNA that marks them as God's renewal agents in a post-pandemic generation that's gone spiritually numb.

Here are seven defining traits of these unlikely but Spirit-empowered leaders:

1. They Carry Holy Discontent

Remnant leaders are not content with complacency. They carry a deep ache for more—not more noise, programs, or crowds, but more of God's presence. Like Nehemiah, who wept over Jerusalem's ruins (Neh 1:4), they allow God's burden to become their calling. Their discontent isn't grumbling—it's groaning that leads to intercession and action (Rom 8:26–27).

They long for the presence of God to be real, transforming, and contagious. Like Habakkuk, they cry out, "LORD, I have heard of your fame; I stand in awe of your deeds. *Repeat them in our day*" (Hab 3:2; emphasis mine).

Remnant leaders carry a holy discontent. They aren't cynical, but they aren't content with the status quo. They believe that what God has done before, he can do again.

And they prepare the way—not with hype but with hunger.

"You stir us, so that praising you may bring us joy," wrote Augustine.[1] That divine stirring is the spark that ignites remnant leadership.

2. They Lead from Their Knees

Remnant leaders know that revival rarely, if ever, begins in a boardroom—rather, it begins in a prayer room. Their power flows from proximity to God. Like Daniel, who knelt daily despite political danger (Dan 6:10), they anchor their leadership in intimacy, not influence. They carry more authority in secret than many carry in public.

Remnant leaders are grounded in discernment before direction. In a culture obsessed with strategy and visibility, they begin with stillness. Like Elijah on Mount Horeb, they know that God's power is not always in the wind or the fire—but in the whisper (1 Kgs 19:11–13).

They don't rush to speak or act. They don't chase applause or affirmation. They ask, "What is the Spirit saying? What is Jesus doing?" Then they respond. Their posture is prayerful attentiveness, a practiced sensitivity to the Lord's prompting.

"My sheep hear my voice. I know them, and they follow me" (John 10:27).

Their lives say, If God doesn't show up, we have nothing to offer.

---

1. Augustine, *Confessions* 1.1 (Chadwick, 3).

3. They Are Resilient Through Refining

Pain is part of the preparation for remnant leaders. Joseph endured betrayal, injustice, and years of obscurity before God raised him to leadership (Gen 37–50). Similarly, remnant leaders walk through fire, not around it. Their scars become their strength. They don't just have opinions—they have stories, and those stories carry the fragrance of endurance.

Many remnant leaders have known great suffering. Their strength has been shaped in the fire of trials—loss, failure, grief, betrayal. Like Jacob wrestling at the Jabbok, they emerge blessed but limping. Their leadership doesn't come from ego but from encounter (Gen 32:22–32).

Corrie ten Boom, who survived Ravensbrück and still preached forgiveness.[2] Susanna Wesley, who endured poverty, loss, and illness while raising children who would spark spiritual awakening.[3] Paul, who bore a "thorn in the flesh" and yet declared God's grace sufficient (2 Cor 12:7–10). Remnant saints lead with the humility that is born out of hardship.

They do not boast in success—they boast in weakness because that's where Christ's power is most visible (2 Cor 12:9). Their influence deepens not in spite of hardship but because of how they've allowed God to shape them through it.

4. They Value the Hidden Places

In a world that chases platforms, remnant leaders value the secret place. Like Anna the prophetess, who worshiped and prayed in the temple for decades before holding the Christ child (Luke 2:36–38), they know God does some of his most important work in quiet obscurity. They don't resent the hidden seasons. They embrace them as sacred ground.

---

2. See her story in Ten Boom, *Hiding Place*.

3. Wallace, *Susanna Wesley*. The author provides many more details on her life.

Remnant leaders are not always institutionally secure. Many serve on the edges—administrative assistants, mechanics, bi-vocational pastors, house church shepherds, camp counselors, nurses, mentors, and missionaries. Their lives are rooted in Christ but flexible in structure. They are a modern-day Paul, or Priscilla and Aquila, or Phoebe, or Gaius, deeply invested but free to follow God wherever he leads.

Their posture is both faithful and nimble. They understand that the kingdom isn't limited to platforms or programs. It flourishes wherever people live by faith.

This humility doesn't mean they never lead publicly—but it does mean they're not addicted to visibility. They lead best because they've been led long in private.

5. They Multiply, Not Just Maintain

Remnant leaders don't cling to control; they raise up others. They live with a multiplying mindset, discipling those around them with the urgency of Jesus' Great Commission. Like Paul mentoring Timothy or Elijah passing his mantle to Elisha, they know legacy is not built by guarding influence but by giving it away.

The remnant knows that spiritual legacy is more important than personal leadership. They prioritize raising up others—especially younger believers or those overlooked by the mainstream. Like Paul mentoring Timothy, or Lois and Eunice shaping his faith (2 Tim 1:5), they see discipleship not as optional but essential.

They do not hoard influence. They give it away. They sow seeds into the next generation, trusting that God will water and grow the harvest.

They don't just lead crowds—they pour into people. I'll talk more about this in the next chapter.

6. They Listen for God's Voice over the Crowd's Applause

Like Jeremiah, who prophesied unpopular truth in a nation addicted to comfort (Jer 1), remnant leaders are tuned to the whisper of God even when it contradicts the shout of culture. They walk in conviction, not consensus. They're more concerned with obedience than outcome, trusting that God will honor the path of righteousness even if it's narrow.

They don't look impressive necessarily, by human standards. They're rarely in the spotlight. But remnant leaders live differently. They carry themselves with a quiet gravity, a kind of spiritual weightiness that's hard to define but unmistakable when you're near it. These are the individuals who have been formed in the hidden places—by prayer, pain, and persistence. Their posture isn't loud or flashy; it's kneeling, listening, waiting, and moving in step with the Spirit.

They are culture-aware but kingdom-led.

7. They Love the Church, Even When It's Messy

Remnant leaders do not abandon the Bride when she's bruised. Like Jesus, who wept over Jerusalem and still walked toward the cross, they lean in even when it's painful. They grieve over sin, injustice, and division, but they stay rooted in love and hope. They believe the church is still God's "Plan A"—and they serve that church with gritty grace.

They don't critique from the sidelines—they wash feet in the trenches.

The posture of the remnant isn't a checklist—it's a way of inhabiting the world.

MODERN THREADS OF RENEWAL

God often does his deepest work through disciples who feel least qualified—those who walk quietly but carry great spiritual weight. These "remnant leaders" rarely draw attention to themselves, but their obedience ignites renewal that ripples far beyond them. Take, for example, these illustrations:

The Hush Harbor Churches of the Antebellum South

During the era of slavery in America, enslaved Africans, who were forbidden to gather openly for worship, created secret "hush harbors" in woods and swamps. Under threat of brutal punishment, they prayed, sang spirituals, and preached the liberating hope of the gospel. These meetings sustained faith through horrific suffering and passed down a legacy of resilience and revival that would shape the Black church for generations. These gatherings were led not by the powerful but by the forgotten—yet they cultivated a faith that would resist injustice and fuel civil rights awakenings a century later.[4]

The Indonesian Revival of the 1960s

In the remote island regions of Indonesia, the Holy Spirit moved in extraordinary ways during the 1960s among humble Christians—many of whom had no formal education or denominational infrastructure. Eyewitnesses report miraculous healings, mass conversions, and even supernatural provisions of food and guidance. These events were birthed through fervent prayer meetings and simple obedience. Missionaries noted that the Indonesian believers often received visions or direct promptings from God and responded without hesitation, sparking house church movements that still bear fruit today.[5]

Movements Among Refugees in Europe

Over the past two decades, refugee crises in Europe—especially in Germany, Greece, and Sweden—have unexpectedly become fertile

---

4. Raboteau, *Slave Religion*, 213–40.
5. Tari, *Like a Mighty Wind*, 26–47.

ground for gospel awakening. Local churches and laypeople began quietly ministering to displaced Muslims from Syria, Afghanistan, and Iran. Through hospitality, discipleship, and the bold faith of new converts, house churches are multiplying. In one city in Germany, a single Bible study for refugees grew into more than twenty church plants.[6] Most of the movement's leaders are recent converts with no theological degrees, just a deep gratitude for Jesus and a desire to share him with others.

You'll also see this posture today:

- A grandmother who leads a prayer group of teenagers every Tuesday night
- A local janitor who reads Scripture aloud over every room he cleans
- A twenty-something worship leader who fasts and prays before rehearsal, believing the Spirit still speaks through music
- A couple who hosts a neighborhood meal every Friday night, simply to love their neighbors with no strings attached

They are not famous. But the kingdom bends around their obedience.

Each of these threads testifies to a consistent truth: when faithful people—regardless of background—submit to the Spirit's leading, the kingdom multiplies. They may not wear the titles or stand on the stages, but these everyday saints are God's chosen instruments of renewal.

HOW TO WALK IN THE SPIRIT AS A REMNANT LEADER

Being Spirit-fueled doesn't mean being loud, weird, or super-spiritual. It means being surrendered—daily. Here are three practices that sustain Spirit-fueled life:

---

6. Adeney, *Kingdom Without Borders*, 162–68.

1. Create Space

You can't hear the Spirit if your life is all noise. Practice silence. Fast from distraction. Open your hands in prayer and say, "Come, Holy Spirit."

2. Obey Promptings

Start saying yes to small nudges: text someone, pray with a co-worker, step into a leadership role you don't feel ready for. The Spirit speaks most often in motion.

3. Stay in Step

Galatians 5:25 says, "Since we live by the Spirit, let us keep in step with the Spirit." That implies rhythm, attention, movement. It's a dance, not a checklist.

In chapter 6, we'll explore what happens when the remnant doesn't retreat but multiplies—and how disciple-making is the engine of every true renewal.

REFLECTION AND RENEWAL

Scriptures for Meditation

Acts 1:4–8—Wait and receive the Spirit.

Acts 2:1–4—Pentecost fire.

Acts 4:23–31—Boldness through prayer.

Gal 5:16–26—Walking by the Spirit.

Reflection Questions

1. Are there areas in your leadership or life where you've been relying more on self-effort than on the Spirit?

2. How have you experienced the Spirit's presence or prompting recently?
3. What's one bold step God might be asking you to take—not from fear but by faith?
4. How could your church or community create more space for dependence on the Spirit?

Practice This Week

- Begin each morning with a simple prayer: "Holy Spirit, fill me and lead me today."
- Choose a twenty-four-hour media fast and spend that time in silence or listening prayer.
- Invite someone into a Spirit-fueled conversation—ask how they've experienced God lately and listen with openness.

CHAPTER 6

Multiplying from the Margins
How Remnant Renewal Always Reproduces

As I started at Saint Paul's Church in 2016, I knew I couldn't lead lasting change alone. The congregation was hungry for something deeper, but like many churches, we needed more than inspiration—we needed a discipleship pipeline that would grow leaders from within.

So, I prayed. I asked God not just for programs or plans but for people—specifically, a few people I could invest in who would in turn invest in others. Over time, in conversations, meetings, and hallway moments, I began to notice a handful of guys who either showed leadership or had untapped potential. Some were seasoned believers. Others were renewed in faith. Together, they carried a spiritual curiosity and emotional honesty that signaled they were ready for more.

Eventually, seven of them agreed to join a group I was starting. I called it a "huddle"[1]—not quite a Bible study, not exactly a leadership cohort but a space where we could be real, pray deeply, open the word, and stretch each other as disciples and leaders. I made it clear from day one: this group wasn't just for us. One of

---

1. Adapted from Mike Breen's premise in *Building a Discipling Culture*.

our goals by year's end would be to multiply—to each begin a similar group of our own.

We met weekly for the first couple months, and then biweekly afterwards. And we met in my home—to give it a personal, safe feel. Sometimes we dug into Scripture. Sometimes we simply shared where we were struggling and prayed over each other. Leadership principles emerged naturally—from the lives of Jesus and the early church, from our experiences in ministry, and from the ordinary crucible of everyday life.

By the end of that year, something had clicked. These weren't just seven guys in a group anymore—they were men ready to invest in others.[2] In year two, they either launched their own huddles or co-led with someone else. Seven turned into nearly fifty.

The next year, we multiplied again Leaders were emerging organically—not just from recruitment posters or sign-up sheets but through life-on-life discipleship and invitation. Since then, we've seen well over one hundred people participate in our small group network—intentional gatherings where people are equipped to follow Jesus and help others do the same.

Looking back, I'm now fully convinced that movement doesn't require masses. It starts with a few who are deeply formed, willing to pour into others, and committed to multiplying what they've received.

---

2. I started with just men for a couple of strategic reasons: first, I really didn't know anyone and the first people to respond positively were men; and second, since we were meeting in my home in an intentionally small group experience, I did not want to challenge any ethical boundary lines especially while I was still building trust with the congregation. My congregation had a history of several boundary violations in the past from key leaders, so I was intentionally sensitive to creating a safe environment for growth while trust was built. The second year and beyond, all groups were mixed in terms of gender and age demographics.

THE PATTERN OF REPRODUCTION: DISCIPLES WHO MAKE DISCIPLES

What happened through those small groups wasn't just a strategy—it was a spiritual pattern that traces back to the earliest days of the church. From the call of the first disciples to the explosion of the church in Acts, multiplication has always been the lifeblood of gospel movements.

When Jesus called Peter and Andrew by the sea, he didn't just invite them to follow—he cast a vision for reproduction: "Follow me, and I will make you fishers of people" (Matt 4:19).

Jesus modeled a pattern of investment in a few for the sake of the many. He taught the crowds, but he discipled the Twelve. And even among the Twelve, he spent more time with Peter, James, and John—knowing that transformation in a few deeply rooted hearts would ripple outward.

After the resurrection, Jesus reaffirmed the call to multiply: "Go therefore and make disciples of all nations" (Matt 28:19).

The Greek verb for "make disciples" (*matheteusate*) is the central command of that Great Commission. Jesus wasn't asking for converts. He was commissioning disciple-makers.

The early church followed that call. Acts 2 tells us that those who were baptized and filled with the Spirit "devoted themselves to the apostles' teaching and to fellowship, to the breaking of bread and to prayer" (v. 42). But the fruit of that devotion was not stagnation—it was reproduction: "The Lord added to their number daily those who were being saved" (v. 47).

Paul followed the same model, especially with Timothy: "And the things you have heard me say in the presence of many witnesses, entrust to reliable people who will also be qualified to teach others" (2 Tim 2:2). That's four generations of disciple-making in one verse: Paul discipled Timothy, Timothy discipled "reliable people," "reliable people" discipled others.

Multiplication isn't a modern growth hack—it's the biblical expectation of a healthy, reproducing church.

Yet today, many churches operate more like spiritual holding tanks than launch pads. In fact, many experience a "failure to launch" that sabotages the missional directive. We talk a good game, for sure, saying that we want to reach new people for Jesus, but the expectation of how that outreach will occur often is placed solely on the job description of the pastor. We end up measuring attendance instead of reproduction. We celebrate large events more than spiritual formation. And inevitably we reinforce our own status quo.

But in every true movement of God, discipleship reproduces itself. Leaders multiply. The remnant grows—not through gimmicks or hype but through intentional, Spirit-empowered relationships. Take a look at a few biblical examples.

BIBLICAL CASE STUDIES IN MULTIPLICATION

Jesus and the Seventy-Two (Luke 10:1–17)

While the twelve disciples often take center stage, Jesus also appointed seventy-two others and "sent them two by two ahead of him to every town and place where he was about to go" (Luke 10:1). These weren't casual followers—they were commissioned workers. Jesus didn't just preach; he prepared leaders and multiplied his mission way before the pivotal events of his crucifixion and resurrection.

This was multiplication before Pentecost. Jesus told them to pray for more workers (v. 2), rely on God's provision (vv. 3–8), proclaim peace (v. 5), and heal the sick (v. 9). When they returned rejoicing, he affirmed not just their fruitfulness but their eternal identity: "Rejoice that your names are written in heaven" (v. 20). Their impact flowed from their connection to him.

Our takeaway: Multiplication begins when leaders are equipped and sent—not just when they're perfect. Jesus empowered others early and trusted the Spirit to shape them along the way. That speaks so much hope to me personally!

Priscilla and Aquila (Acts 18:24–28)

Priscilla and Aquila were a married couple, tentmakers by trade, and key figures in Paul's network of ministry. When they encountered Apollos—a gifted preacher who apparently had gaps in his theology—they "invited him to their home and explained to him the way of God more adequately" (Acts 18:26).

They didn't disqualify him. They didn't yell at him. They didn't bar him from preaching. They discipled him.

Apollos went on to become a powerful witness for the gospel in Achaia, "refuting the Jews in public debate, proving from the Scriptures that Jesus was the Messiah" (v. 28). His impact was multiplied because a faithful couple poured into one emerging leader.

Our takeaway: Sometimes, the most catalytic multiplication happens not on stages but in living rooms. Remnant leaders are formed in hospitable spaces and with relational investment.

Paul's Team Model (Rom 16)

In Rom 16, Paul greets more than two dozen people by name—ministry partners, church leaders, risk-takers, and fellow workers. For years, I would skim over this section thinking that it was simply his way of greeting people—"not worth my time," I carelessly and arrogantly thought. What I have come to appreciate about this section, however, is that Paul didn't just write letters or plant churches. He multiplied leaders in every region. This is one of his lists of those leaders—and each one has a story.

Phoebe (v. 1) was likely the courier of the letter and a church leader in Cenchreae. Andronicus and Junia (v. 7) were "outstanding among the apostles." Tryphena and Tryphosa (v. 12) were women who "work hard in the Lord." Paul's list wasn't just a thank-you card—it was a snapshot of remnant leaders who were multiplying the movement.

Our takeaway: Paul didn't build solo ministries; he built ecosystems of multiplying leaders—across backgrounds, genders, and locations. What implications does that have for us in our local congregations?

The Church in Thessalonica (1 Thess 1:6–8)

When you look at this passage through the lens of remnant multiplication, this is truly humbling and inspiring. Paul describes how this young church not only received the gospel with joy despite suffering but "*became a model* to all the believers in Macedonia and Achaia" (v. 7; emphasis mine). He adds, "The Lord's message rang out from you not only in Macedonia and Achaia—your faith in God has become known *everywhere*" (v. 8; emphasis mine).

This wasn't a megachurch. It was a remnant church that caught fire—and multiplied its witness through resilient faith, visible joy, and unshakable commitment.

Our takeaway: You don't need large numbers to spark gospel impact. You need contagious faith and intentional replication.

Does that ignite faith in you? Keep reading.

MODERN THREADS OF RENEWAL: MULTIPLYING MOVEMENTS IN REAL TIME

There are more modern examples as well. Throughout history, renewal has always found momentum through multiplication. What began in obscurity among a few faithful saints grew into movements that reshaped churches, communities, and nations. Here are several modern case studies that illustrate how remnant churches embraced multiplying practices and became catalysts for gospel renewal:

The Kansas City Underground

The Kansas City Underground (KCU) is a decentralized network of missional communities committed to "saturating their city with the gospel." Rather than relying on a centralized Sunday service, they train everyday believers to plant "microchurches"—small, reproducible groups built around mission, discipleship, and worship. KCU's guiding principle is "one missionary per neighborhood." They don't ask how many people attend; they ask how many "live sent" (meaning, how many people are living out their mission to the neighborhoods). Multiplication happens as ordinary people are trained to lead in their own relational networks—whether that's in gyms, coffee shops, or apartment buildings. Their model reflects a New Testament rhythm: simple, Spirit-led, and scalable. Their co-founder Brian Johnson says, "We train people to hear from God and obey what He says in the context of community and mission."[3] The microchurch model is definitely worth exploring more.

The Alpha Course

What began as a small group course at Holy Trinity Brompton (HTB) in London has become a global movement. The Alpha Course invites skeptics, seekers, and new believers into conversations about life, faith, and Jesus. It's intentionally nonthreatening—centered around food, film, and honest questions. Although I've heard of Alpha for years, I really didn't know much about it until I did this research. I'm now quite intrigued! The key to Alpha's multiplication? Reproducibility. Anyone can run it. And every time a course ends, leaders are encouraged to invite guests to co-lead the next round. Over time, this has led to exponential growth—Alpha has been run in more than one hundred countries and translated into more than a hundred languages. By emphasizing hospitality, conversation, and relational trust, Alpha embodies a remnant ethos: small circles of faith multiplying outward.[4]

---

3. Ford et al., *Starfish and the Spirit*, 74–75.
4. Alpha USA, "What Is Alpha?"

The Filipino Church Planting Movement

In the Philippines, a powerful church planting movement has taken root—not through celebrity leaders but through ordinary believers trained to multiply disciples and communities. Church Multiplication Coalition (CMC), among other networks, equips laypeople to start simple churches in homes, workplaces, and unreached neighborhoods. These churches multiply rapidly by using Discovery Bible Study (similar to Alpha), local leadership development, and a clear discipleship pathway. Their strategy is built on 2 Tim 2:2—entrust the gospel to reliable people who will teach others. Their basic principle is that they focus not just on how many people each leader is reaching but how many they are equipping to reach whole neighborhoods. Today, there are thousands of small churches planted through these decentralized efforts—reminding us that multiplying the mission is still God's method for awakening the world.[5]

CORE PRACTICES THAT FUEL MULTIPLICATION

Multiplying churches and movements don't grow because of gimmicks—they grow because of faithful practices. Remnant renewal is sustained and multiplied through rhythms that are deeply rooted, not flashy. These include the following:

1. Prayerful Dependence

Before movements multiply, they are birthed in prayer. The Moravians launched a hundred-year prayer meeting. The early church gathered in an upper room. Your church may start with a living room, but if prayer is present, power will follow.

Way too many of our churches are under-prayed. I'm not sure why. Prayer is the crucible within which the Holy Spirit

---

5. See Church Multiplication Coalition, *International Manual*.

forms character, stirs new life, creates vision, empowers witness, and breaks strongholds. Yet, notoriously we congregations and our leaders are content to keep prayer as an opener to the "real agenda" of our meetings, a brief offering in our worship services so as not to turn off any visitors (yes, that was actually a strategy in the church growth movement of the late 1990s), or something that we do only in times of illness, trauma, or desperation.

Prayer is the main communication connection we have with our heavenly Father. When we're not praying, we're not depending on him for the necessary equipping to carry out his mission of multiplying the kingdom. Jesus reminded his disciples, "I am the vine; you are the branches. If you remain in me and I in you, you will bear much fruit; *apart from me you can do nothing*" (John 15:5; emphasis mine).

2. Discipleship That Reproduces

Too many churches also settle for programmatic discipleship. But multiplication requires relational, reproducing discipleship. Jesus didn't hand out certificates—he invested in people who would invest in others.

If the remnant is to equip a movement, we need to focus on discipleship no matter the context. On the upper right corner of the white board in the office area where our staff meets, I have written, "*Everything is about making disciples. Everything.*" It's been there since I arrived at this church in 2016 as a daily reminder that God never wastes any opportunity to equip his people to know and love him, and to share the good news in all circumstances. The good, the bad, and the ugly, they're all opportunities for discipleship—for deepening our connection to the Lord of life.

3. Empowering Everyday Saints

Revived remnants release the ministry to the people. In Eph 4:12, Paul teaches that leaders exist "to equip the saints for the work of ministry." Multiplication happens when every believer sees themselves as a minister.

In my book *Mission Rift*, I go into greater detail about how the "pastor-centered model of ministry" is not only unbiblical, but it also has been contributing to the slow decline of modern Christianity—so I won't go into details here.[6] But I will say that when the remnant feels empowered to live and serve within the full range of God's giftings, multiplication becomes exponential in potential.

4. Leadership Pipeline, Not Pulpit Bottleneck

A remnant church raises up the next generation of leaders—not just to fill vacancies but to extend the mission.

Back to my home church. When I was sixteen years old, I was the president of my youth group (a total of four teenagers). As we met, we thought it would be a great idea to have a "Youth Sunday," where we would lead the worship service, preach the message, read the Bible passages, and offer the prayers. We presented our idea to the pastor and he readily agreed. The Sunday prior to our debut, the pastor came to me with a manila envelop with my name on it.

"What's this?" I asked.

"It's your sermon for next week," the pastor said.

"My sermon? But I've been working on my sermon for the past few weeks; I'm just about done."

"Oh, that's not going to work," he replied. "You see, you're not licensed to preach, so this is the message that you'll be giving. It's all typed up."

"But I thought the point of 'Youth Sunday' was that the *youth* would lead the service. We're planning on doing the message and reading the Scriptures and offering the prayers and..."

The pastor cut me off. "Oh, you can't read the Scriptures either since you haven't been trained. I'll be here to do that for you."

---

6. Woolverton, *Mission Rift*, 101.

In a moment of teenage frustration, I looked at him and said, "But you're not a youth." It was then that I cancelled Youth Sunday.

It was also then that I disengaged from my desire to be a part of that church.

Multiplication is hindered when leadership is hoarded.

5. Open Hands, Open Doors

Churches that multiply aren't territorial. They celebrate equipping and sending. When God raised up Barnabas and Paul, the church at Antioch laid hands on them and sent them on missionary journeys (Acts 13). That's the spirit of multiplication.

As a leader, I like hiring great staff to be a part of our team. When I find a good person, I pour into them, intentionally equipping them to increase their capacity for greater leadership. After doing so, inevitably they would then leave to go to other ministry venues requiring me to begin the process all over again. For years this was a major source of frustration for me: "I pour myself into these people for the benefit of our mission and ministries, so why do they keep leaving?!"

It took me a while to realize that my role was to "mentor and multiply for the sake of the kingdom," not necessarily solely for the local church. God had placed me in positions to equip those whom he was calling to influence other contexts. I've learned to live by an "open hands, open doors" philosophy that in the moment may fuel my frustrations for staffing my team but ultimately humbles me by how God has used me to advance his greater mission.

Remnant leaders expect a larger return on their investment in others. And that return is based on a mission that is bigger than our own.

A MOVEMENT WITHIN REACH

The temptation for tired churches is to aim for maintenance, not movement. But God revives his remnant to multiply—not because the church needs to grow but because the world needs to be reached. You may feel small, unnoticed, or under-resourced. I get it—I've been there. But remember—mustard seeds, loaves and fishes, and one hundred and twenty disciples in an upper room all sparked global impact.

God doesn't just revive people for their sake. He revives them to be sent.

Up next in chapter 7, we'll explore how remnant churches can't help but tell the life-changing story of how Jesus has impacted their lives. Practical evangelism in today's culture—the natural flow of passionate story telling.

REFLECTION AND RENEWAL

Scriptures for Meditation

> Matt 28:19-20—"Go therefore and make disciples of all nations."
>
> 2 Tim 2:2—"Entrust to reliable people who will also be qualified to teach others."
>
> Luke 16:10—"Whoever is faithful in very little..."
>
> Acts 6:7—"The number of disciples in Jerusalem increased rapidly."
>
> John 15:8—"This is to my Father's glory, that you bear much fruit."

Reflection Questions

1. In what areas has your church prioritized preservation over multiplication?
2. Which of the "core practices" above could you begin integrating this month?
3. Who in your life might God be calling you to disciple, release, or send?

Practice This Week

Remnant renewal doesn't end with personal revival—it grows when you give it away. It's the paradox of Jesus' teaching.

This week, I encourage you prayerfully to take one small, intentional step toward multiplication in your circle of influence. Here's how you might begin:

1. Ask God to Show You Who to Pour Into

Begin with prayer. Ask yourself, "Who in my circles of influence could benefit from my investment in them?" Look for someone curious about faith, growing in leadership, or eager for deeper discipleship. You don't need to know everything—just be willing to walk with them.

"The harvest is plentiful, but the workers are few. Ask the Lord of the harvest . . ." (Luke 10:2).

2. Choose One Way to Start Multiplying

Multiplication doesn't need a stage. Try one of these steps:

- Invite someone to read Scripture with you weekly.
- Start a short-term group to discuss a book or topic of faith.
- Ask someone to co-lead or apprentice in your current small group or ministry—or perhaps invite them to join you on a short-term mission trip.
- Share your story of faith with someone in a personal conversation.
- Equip a newer believer to start discipling someone else.

3. Resist the "Too Small to Matter" Lie

The enemy loves to whisper that your influence is too limited, your circle too narrow, or your efforts too weak. Don't believe it! Remnant renewal has always started small. God's pattern is yeast in dough, seeds in soil, loaves and fish in a hungry crowd.

"Do not despise these small beginnings, for the Lord rejoices to see the work begin." (Zech 4:10 NLT).

4. Revisit the Discipleship Mandate

Spend a few minutes meditating on Matt 28:18–20. Ask the Spirit to renew your sense of calling—not just to follow Jesus but to help others follow him too. Consider journaling your reflections as you engage the text:

- Who has multiplied into you? What did they do that helped you grow?
- Who might you invest in now—starting with one intentional conversation or invitation this week?

CHAPTER 7

Awakened to the Gospel
The Remnant Tells the Story with Passion

ONE OF MY FAVORITE things to do used to be writing my sermons at a Barnes & Noble café. Arriving every Thursday morning with my Bible, notebook, and a prayer—"Lord, where do you want me to sit today, and who do you want me to meet?"—I would plant myself at a spot, grab a drink from the barista, begin my study time, and wait on how the Spirit would work in building connections. Almost every time, God would orchestrate a moment—someone would sit nearby and we'd find ourselves in a conversation about life, faith, or struggles. Over the years, these moments shaped my understanding of evangelism—not as a scripted exchange but as a posture of listening, discerning, and trusting the Spirit's guidance.

When I moved to a new church, I lost my café routine, but the Spirit's nudging didn't stop. Whether at a restaurant with my pastoral team or in a grocery store checkout, I learned that God could open doors anywhere.

One day at a grocery store, I noticed the cashier's large cross tattoo. That was my open door. "Does that cross have meaning for you?" I asked. Over several weeks, our brief exchanges turned into something more. I learned his name—Josh—and began praying for him regularly, even though our conversations weren't particularly deep at first. But evangelism often starts small—earning trust, building a connection, allowing space for spiritual curiosity to grow.

Josh eventually introduced me to his girlfriend, Amy, who had attended my church as a child. She was pregnant, and Josh confided in me that he was trying to get his life together for the baby's sake. He had been in prison for a short time, struggled with alcohol, and feared he wasn't capable of being a good father. "I want to be better," he said one day, after months of casual conversations.

Then came the breaking point. Late one evening, my phone rang. It was Josh, distraught. He had gone out drinking with friends and had come home drunk. Amy was furious, threatening to kick him out and prevent him from seeing their baby. His shame was palpable. "I screwed up," he sobbed. "I don't know how to fix it."

We met the next morning, and he unloaded his regrets. "I keep trying, but I keep failing," he said. "I want to change. I just don't know how."

I sat in silence for a moment, praying internally, asking God for the right words. Then, I leaned in.

"Josh, I see how much you care about Amy and your son. I see how much you want to do right by them. But change doesn't happen just by trying harder—it happens when we surrender. You need something more than willpower. You need Jesus."

His head dropped into his hands. "I know," he whispered. "I just don't know if he would want me."

"He does," I assured him. "He already does. He loves you—not because you've earned it but because that's who he is."

Josh's tears fell freely now. "I want this," he said. "I want Jesus."

We prayed together, and right there in my office, he surrendered his life to Christ. When we finished, he exhaled, like he had been holding his breath for years. The weight was gone.

Three weeks later, he stood in front of the church, ready to be baptized. He wore a somewhat wrinkled white shirt (the shirt he wore to work—the only "dressy" shirt he had) and a tie I had given him—his way of marking the significance of the day. And he had brought his entire family—Amy, their son, Josh's parents,

Amy's mom. While I was introducing him to the congregation, he jumped out of his seat, ran up to me, and hugged me, sobbing.

"Do you confess Jesus Christ as your Lord and Savior?" I asked, as he calmed himself and we began the baptism.

"YES!" he shouted.

With each baptism question, his voice grew stronger, his excitement tangible. As the water of baptism dripped down his face, mingling with his tears, the entire congregation was caught in the beauty and sounds of grace.

Evangelism isn't clean or predictable. It's messy. It's built on relationships, Spirit-led nudges, and a willingness to walk alongside people in their struggles. And sometimes, it's as simple as noticing a tattoo, starting a conversation, and trusting that God is already at work.

That's the remnant way. Not polished. But powerful.

Telling the story of Jesus has never been a performance—it's always been personal. And when God's remnant is awakened to the reality of the gospel, they can't help but share it. Evangelism, at its core, isn't a duty—it's the overflow of a transformed life.

BIBLICAL REMNANT WITNESSES: SET FREE AND SENT OUT

Throughout Scripture, ordinary people who encountered Jesus couldn't keep quiet. They didn't have degrees or training—but they had a story. And it was enough.

The Gerasene Demoniac (Mark 5:1–20)

After being delivered from a legion of demons, the man begged to follow Jesus. But Jesus said, "Go home to your own people and *tell them how much the Lord has done for you*" (v. 19; emphasis mine). He did—and the Decapolis was never the same.

The Samaritan Woman (John 4:1–42)

With a messy past and questionable reputation, she became one of the first evangelists. She left her water jar and ran back to town, telling anyone who'd listen, "Come see a man who told me everything I ever did" (v. 29). Many believed because of her witness.

The Blind Man Healed at Siloam (John 9)

When the religious leaders interrogated him, all he could say was, "I was blind, but now I see" (v. 25). His unshakable testimony confounded the elite and drew others to Jesus.

The Philippian Jailer (Acts 16:25–34)

After Paul and Silas were freed by an earthquake, they stayed in their prison cell—leading the jailer and his whole household to faith. One night. One act of mercy. A family changed forever.

Paul, Formerly Saul (Acts 9, 22; Gal 1)

Once a persecutor of Christians, his radical encounter with Jesus fueled a life of bold witness. Everywhere he went, he told his story—of grace that pursued even the most unlikely.

What these people had in common wasn't perfection. It was passion. They didn't quote doctrinal positions or systematic theology. They shared what they knew: "This is what Jesus did for me."

PRACTICAL EVANGELISM IN A POST-CHRISTIAN CULTURE

Evangelism today doesn't look like it did fifty years ago—and that's a good thing. In a post-Christian world, people aren't asking, "How can I be saved?" They're asking, "Why should I trust you?"

Before people are ready to hear about Jesus, they want to see that he's changed you—and that you care.

Remnant leaders don't lead with pressure. They lead with presence. Gospel witness in our time must be relational, discerning, and responsive to the Spirit.

Here are five core practices that have helped me to cultivate a natural, passionate gospel witness in today's culture—perhaps you can add more:

1. Live Your Story, Then Share It

Your personal story is one of the most powerful tools God has given you. You don't need to have a dramatic conversion or seminary degree—you just need to be honest. People are drawn not to perfection but to transformation.

Ask yourself the following:

- Who was I before Jesus?
- What changed when I met him?
- What is God doing in my life right now?

Keep your story simple and human. Instead of focusing on doctrine first, focus on personal change. A young professional once shared with a coworker, "Honestly, I used to find my identity in achievement. But over time, my faith in Jesus started to show me I didn't have to earn worth—I already had it in him." That coworker later asked to attend church with him.

Our challenge: Write out a three-minute version of your testimony. Keep it conversational. Practice it aloud—not to perfect it but to own it.

2. Start with Listening

Evangelism is not about having all the answers. It starts with asking good questions and listening without an agenda. Jesus modeled this beautifully. With the woman at the well, he began with a request: "Will you give me a drink?" (John 4:7). He didn't lead with theology. He led with curiosity.

In today's culture, people long to be seen and heard. When you listen to their stories, you earn the right to speak into them.

Listening for Values

- Pay attention to what people celebrate, complain about, or dream of. Those are value indicators.
- A parent who says, "I just want my kids to be safe and loved" is expressing a value that connects directly to God's heart.
- A friend struggling with purpose might say, "I feel like I'm just drifting." That opens a door to speak about calling and identity in Christ.

Our challenge: Practice asking open-ended questions like, "What's been giving you hope lately?" or "How have you been processing everything going on in the world?" Don't pivot too quickly to your faith—let the Spirit lead the timing.

3. Practice Hospitality

Hospitality is a lost art—and a powerful witness. When you open your life and table to others, you make the gospel tangible. In Scripture, meals were often the setting for healing, teaching, and reconciliation.

Hospitality is more than entertaining. It's about making space for others to belong before they believe.

For example: Growing up, my grandmother would welcome everyone in the family to her house on Christmas Eve for what the Italians would call "the feast of seven fishes." We packed into her basement, sitting side by side with others that she had invited—the mailman, the neighbors up the street, and even the homeless guy who hung out on the corner. Her crowded basement became a sweet space where food, friendship, and love broke down walls.

When grandma no longer could do the meal, my mom and dad took over. Through the years, the feast of seven fishes became a tradition of welcoming others who had no specific plans for dinner on this holy night. It was quite common for our tables to be filled with police officers, the Muslim owners of a local restaurant and their family, my parents' Jewish doctor, a nurse or two from the local hospital, salespeople from the Hallmark store nearby where they shopped—all invited and welcomed to sit at the table as "family."

In later years, during the course of the evening, inevitably my mom would ask me to "offer communion"—saying, "it's something we should do." Now, I know all the doctrinal reasons why this might not be appropriate at such a setting, but it was always a way to introduce Jesus into the conversation—perhaps my mom's unspoken agenda. Wanting to honor her request but also a sacramental theology, I provided a modified "love feast."

And it worked every time. Churched, non-churched, Christian, non-Christian, family, stranger—we paused at the end of the meal to look at life through a different lens. Abundant food, a warm welcome, and a love that poked itself through the walls that normally separated us—all created a space where it was safe to talk about life, faith, and hope.

Our challenge: Choose one person or family this month to invite for a meal. Don't overcomplicate it. A pizza night with your kids playing nearby can be just as sacred as a candlelit dinner. Simply open your life to what God might have in mind.

4. Serve with No Strings Attached

Jesus healed, fed, and comforted long before people called him Lord. In a skeptical world, service is often more powerful than sermons. Acts of love tend to disarm cynicism and open pathways for relationships, healing, and the restoration of hope. They also tend to reproduce themselves—a "pay-it-forward" kind of momentum.

Practical Ideas

- Pay for someone's coffee and say, "Just wanted to pass on some love today. God's been kind to me."
- Offer childcare for a single parent who's exhausted.
- Volunteer at a community event, not to get attention but to reflect Christ's heart.

An illustration: A high school teacher I know once kept granola bars in her desk for students who skipped breakfast. When I asked her why she did this, she said, "God sees my students even when it feels like no one else does." Students started asking more about her faith—not because she preached but because she paid attention.

Our challenge: Make a list of the natural circles where you already live—work, neighborhood, gym, school. Ask, "Where could I quietly reflect God's kindness here?"

5. Know When to Speak—and When Not To

This may be the most underrated evangelism skill: discernment.

Jesus didn't always answer questions—sometimes he asked more. He stayed silent before Pilate. He walked away from some crowds. Evangelism isn't about winning arguments. It's about recognizing moments where hearts are open—and being okay when they're not. This was such a key learning for me.

When to speak: When someone shows vulnerability, asks questions, or reflects spiritual hunger—step in with grace and clarity. Start by sharing your story, not doctrine. We don't feed steak to a newborn.

When not to speak: When someone is defensive, mocking, or emotionally closed off—stay curious, kind, and patient. You're sowing seeds. Let the Spirit do the work.

How to Transition a Conversation Gently

- Instead of, "Let me tell you about Jesus," try, "Can I share something that helped me when I was in a similar place?"
- Instead of, "You need church," try, "We've found our church to be a real lifeline during hard times—if you ever want to come, let me know."

An illustration: One of my church members shared with me that a business colleague at his company came to him one day and said, "I see how you keep your calm under pressure. What's your secret?" My church member responded, "Honestly, my faith keeps me centered. I believe God is at work even in chaos." That sparked a deeper conversation weeks later when that same colleague faced a family crisis. A seed was planted that later took root.

Our takeaway: Pray each morning, "Lord, help me be sensitive to your Spirit and open to divine appointments. Who do you want me to encounter today?" Don't force doors open—but don't ignore them either.

REFLECTION AND SMALL GROUP PROMPTS

Consider your own story. Allow these reflection questions to guide you in developing a path toward remnant multiplication.

1. What's Your Story?

How would you describe your journey with Jesus in under three minutes? What part of your story do you think someone else needs to hear?

2. Who's in Front of You?

Who are one or two people in your life right now who might be spiritually curious but not yet connected to faith or church? How can you start listening more deeply?

3. When Have You Been Served by Love?

Share a time when someone's kindness pointed you to Jesus—or planted a seed. What did you learn from that experience?

4. Where Is God Already at Work?

Think about your workplace, neighborhood, or school. Where do you sense the Spirit opening hearts? What's one small step you could take to join in?

5. What Keeps You Silent?

Is it fear? Uncertainty? Worry you'll say the wrong thing? What truth about God might help you move forward with grace and boldness?

6. How Can You Create Space for Others?

Where can you extend hospitality—your home, a coffee shop, a lunch break? What would it look like to lead with invitation rather than persuasion?

MODERN REMNANT STORIES

There are numerous examples of remnant individuals who are passionate about evangelism in modern times. Consider these two illustrations:

Andrew Palau and Festival Evangelism[1]

The son of Luis Palau didn't initially want to follow in his father's footsteps. But after a personal renewal in his twenties, Andrew embraced his call to preach. Through global city festivals, he shares the gospel with joy, relevance, and clarity—reaching people from all walks of life. I receive emails regularly from his organization.

The Chosen Series and Media Witness

Created by Dallas Jenkins, *The Chosen* reimagines the gospel narrative through the lens of storytelling. It's a modern witness—shared not in a church but through screens. Millions have seen Jesus afresh because someone dared to tell the story creatively.

What about you?

In chapter 8, we'll explore what it means to be resilient in opposition—how God uses hardship, rejection, and even failure to deepen and spread the work of renewal.

REFLECTION AND RENEWAL

Scriptures for Meditation

Mark 5:1–20—The delivered man's mission begins at home.

John 4:1–42—The Samaritan woman shares her encounter.

Acts 1:8—"You will be my witnesses."

2 Cor 5:20—"We are ambassadors for Christ."

Rom 1:16—"I am not ashamed of the gospel."

Reflection Questions

1. Who in your life shared the gospel with passion and authenticity? How did it impact you?

---

1. Palau, *Secret Life*, for more background on his life.

2. What holds you back from sharing your story more freely?
3. Where is God already opening a door for gospel conversations?
4. What would it look like to live as a remnant witness in your workplace, neighborhood, or family?

Practice This Week

Think back on your journey with Jesus. What are three ways your life has changed because of him? Write them down. Then ask God to give you one opportunity this week to share even a part of that story—with a friend, coworker, or family member.

You don't need the perfect words. You just need a willing heart.

CHAPTER 8

Opposition and the Remnant Leader

SPIRITUAL RENEWAL NEVER GOES UNCONTESTED. Wherever God stirs revival, resistance follows. Sometimes it's external—cultural pushback, church politics, or spiritual warfare. Other times, the struggle is within—our own fears, pride, or burnout quietly sabotaging what God is building.

Opposition isn't a detour from the journey of renewal. It *is* the journey.

THE LONE PROPHET: MICAIAH'S STAND

The scene in 1 Kgs 22 is electric with tension. King Ahab of Israel is plotting war against Ramoth-Gilead, and he wants the favor of heaven—or at least the illusion of it. So, he gathers four hundred prophets who deliver exactly what he wants to hear: "Go, for the Lord will give it into the king's hand" (v. 6). Everything sounds victorious, but something about the unanimous chorus seems off to Jehoshaphat, the king of Judah. He asks Ahab, "Is there no longer a prophet of the LORD here whom we can inquire of?" (v. 7).

Reluctantly, Ahab names Micaiah. "But I hate him," Ahab confesses, "because he never prophesies anything good about me, but always bad" (v. 8). Still, Micaiah is summoned. On his way, he's warned to say what everyone else is saying—to go along to get along. But when the moment comes, Micaiah refuses to echo the crowd. He declares what God actually said: that Ahab will be defeated and the people will be scattered like sheep without a shepherd (v. 17).

A slap across the face and a prison sentence follow. Micaiah is thrown in jail and given bread and water until Ahab returns—which, as Micaiah had prophesied, never happens (vv. 24–27). He speaks truth, knowing it won't be received, and suffers for it.

Micaiah's courage in the face of groupthink shows us a remnant truth: the louder the applause for power, the higher the cost for the voice that confronts it. Remnant leaders often find themselves outnumbered, overlooked, or punished for their faithfulness. But like Micaiah, they remain anchored in the word of the Lord.

RESISTANCE AS THE REMNANT'S REALITY

Opposition isn't the exception for remnant leaders—it's the expectation.

From the beginning, God's messengers have faced not only cultural resistance but internal backlash from within their own people. When Moses rose to lead, his authority was constantly questioned, even by family (Num 12). When Jeremiah prophesied to Judah, he was beaten and thrown into a cistern (Jer 38). Esther risked everything to approach the king when her people's survival was at stake. Paul, too, was rejected by both his former allies and new brothers.

Jesus himself, though sinless, was resisted by those who knew him best. He was misunderstood by his family, rejected in his hometown, and eventually crucified by both the people of his own tribe as well as the Romans who, ironically, postured a "love for peace" (Pax Romana). The cross is not the exception for the remnant—it's the pattern.

Repeatedly, the faithful remnant is refined in the fire of resistance. Not always by enemies but often by friendly fire—leaders within the system who feel threatened by change. It's in these moments that the remnant learns the hard truth: comfort and calling rarely go hand in hand.

In Scripture and in history, the pattern is clear: when God awakens a remnant, opposition intensifies. But it's in this furnace that the depth of our discipleship is revealed. As you lead into renewal, expect friction. Not because you're doing something wrong but because you're stepping into what is right.

And yet, resilience is not bravado. It's not willpower. It's spiritual depth formed through surrender, Scripture, and the slow burn of faithful practice. The remnant road is rarely easy. And yet, opposition doesn't cancel the call. It clarifies it.

OPPOSITION REVEALS WHAT COMFORT CONCEALS

Hardship and conflict don't just threaten spiritual renewal—they test it. Opposition unmasks whether the fire we carry is real or borrowed.

In safe, sanitized ministry settings, it's easy to talk about faith. In comfortable settings, we can fake depth of faith. But when crisis or conflict comes, when the pressure mounts, when the fruit is slow, or when you're criticized for following Jesus too closely, only what's rooted in Christ remains. Crisis and conflict always expose the foundations of our faith.

Through the enduring of challenges, resilient remnant leaders develop:

- A theology of suffering
- A practice of prayer
- A community of support
- A commitment to the long view

Resilience is less about toughness and more about trust: in whom or in what will we place our trust and faith?

A resilient remnant leader isn't just a fighter. They're a formed person—someone shaped deeply by the presence of Christ. Remnant leaders are not passive peacekeepers. They're warriors fighting a battle that not everyone sees, not everyone understands, and not everyone supports.

As you negotiate these pivotal conflicts and challenges, here are five practices that spiritually form leaders who can stand when opposition rises.

FIVE PRACTICES OF SPIRITUALLY FORMED REMNANT RESILIENCE

1. Anchor Your Identity in God's Voice

In seasons of opposition, other voices grow loud—critics, culture, even our own insecurities and arrogance. Remnant leaders must return daily to the voice of God. Jesus heard the Father's voice before he ever faced the wilderness (Matt 3:17—4:1). In John 10:27, Jesus reminds us that his sheep hear his voice: "I know them, and they follow me." In his fold, we have the assurance that no one can "snatch" us out of his protective care (John 10:29). Remnant resilience begins with knowing who—and whose—you are and in trusting in God's provision.

Micaiah didn't bend because he wasn't dependent on Ahab's approval. When we are secure in God's calling and voice, we can withstand the noise around us. Remnant leaders return again and again to what God has said—through Scripture, prayer, and trusted community.

Every remnant leader will be misrepresented. What sustains them is not approval but anchored identity: "You are my beloved; with you I am well pleased" (see Luke 3:22)—a moniker for Jesus at his baptism, for sure, but also a reminder to all of us that we are known and loved by the One who has created us and called us. That identity must be received before the battle—and remembered during it. No ministry outcome can define what only the heavenly Father can declare.

2. Embrace the Hidden Life

True strength is formed in secret places. Before Jesus launched his public ministry, he withdrew to the wilderness and into prayer (Luke 5:16). Spiritual resilience requires rhythms of retreat, silence, and soul recalibration.

Why? Because not all opposition is from the enemy. Sometimes it comes from friends, family, or fear. Spiritually resilient leaders learn to ask, "What is God refining in me through this pushback?" We must pull away to listen, to discern, to discover, to confess, to renew, to find strength. The hidden life sustains the public one—otherwise we begin to believe what others say about us and what we say about ourselves, whether good, bad, or ugly.

Spiritual formation begins in obscurity. Jesus spent thirty hidden years before his public ministry began. Resistance often drives us underground—emotionally, socially, or vocationally—but it's in caves and deserts that God specializes in deepening character, perseverance, and inner resolve. Remnant leaders embrace these hidden seasons as sacred ground.

3. Contend in Prayer

Prayer is not the last resort of the weary; it's the battleground of the remnant. True opposition is often spiritual. Contending prayer—persistent, Spirit-led intercession—shifts atmospheres and strengthens the inner life of the leader. The psalmist cried, "When I am afraid, I put my trust in you" (Ps 56:3). Remnant leaders live on their knees.

Opposition demands wisdom, not just will. Remnant leaders must discern whether resistance is demonic, human, systemic—or self-inflicted. Like Jesus in the wilderness, we need Scripture-shaped clarity to respond rightly. Discernment is spiritual vigilance cultivated through regular rhythms of silence, examen, and community counsel.

The remnant way isn't about charging forward at all costs—it's about moving in step with the Spirit. Opposition can tempt us to become reactive or defensive. But discernment listens for God's invitation even in difficulty. As Paul prayed, "That you may discern what is best" (Phil 1:10).

4. Develop Holy Endurance

The writer of Hebrews in our New Testament calls us to "run with endurance the race marked out for us" (Heb 12:1). This isn't gritted-teeth survival. It's Spirit-empowered perseverance rooted in joy, hope, and a long view of God's redemptive work. Endurance is less about pace and more about presence.

Opposition often exposes our limits. That's not failure—it's formation. When Paul's "thorn" wasn't removed, he learned that God's power is perfected in weakness (2 Cor 12:9). Remnant leaders embrace dependence. They need to guard the fire. When culture, fatigue, or failure threatens to douse our calling, we need rather to fan it into flame. Paul gives that advice to his protégé, Timothy: "Fan into flame the gift of God" (2 Tim 1:6).

The word Paul uses in Greek is *anazopyreo*. It appears only once in the New Testament—here in 2 Timothy. It means to rekindle, revive, or stir up.[1] Paul is reminding Timothy that faithfulness to his calling and to the gospel is something that must be cultivated, stoked, nurtured, constantly remembered, and protected—since what that calling and gospel represent is threatening to the enemy of love. Opposition may be able to take away many things but it cannot rob us of our identity and calling in Christ.

Therefore, it's important for us to refuse to be defined by outcomes. Results fluctuate. Faithfulness doesn't. God calls us to obedience, not optics.

---

1. Bauer et al., *Greek-English Lexicon*, s.v. "ἀναζωπυρέω."

5. Stay in the Story

Resilient leaders keep the long view—what I've called "the mosaic view" in my book *Prophet and Loss*.[2] They don't define their story by single chapter (or mosaic tile) of conflict, rejection, or fruitlessness. They trust that even painful scenes serve God's larger narrative. In the fog of failure or the fire of opposition, they whisper, "This is not the end." As Eugene Peterson put it, "a long obedience in the same direction" is what brings fruit.[3]

For us to stay in the story, remnant leaders need to stay embedded in the body of Christ. Isolation is where leaders unravel. Remnant leaders thrive in mutual submission and shared vulnerability. Not just accountability—but belonging. The early church endured persecution by gathering often, breaking bread, and praying together (Acts 2:42–47). You cannot outlast opposition without being held by love within community.

Don't let a hard chapter define the whole narrative. Joseph was sold, slandered, and sidelined before being raised up. Stay faithful in the part of the story you're in. God is always working in the long arc of redemption.

MODERN REMNANT EXAMPLES

Consider these examples from more modern times.

Richard Wurmbrand: Tortured for preaching in Communist Romania, he wrote *Tortured for Christ* from a prison cell. His suffering birthed Voice of the Martyrs, a global network supporting persecuted believers.[4]

The Mother Emanuel AME Church: In 2015, after a white supremacist murdered nine church members during a Bible study, families publicly forgave the killer. Their radical grace stunned the nation and pointed to a power deeper than hate.[5]

---

2. Woolverton, *Prophet and Loss*, 45.
3. A reference to Peterson, *Long Obedience*.
4. Wurmbrand, *Tortured for Christ*, where you can read his story.
5. Elliott et al., "10 Years After." For greater reflection, see also Hawes,

Nabeel Qureshi: A Muslim-background convert and apologist, he battled cancer in his thirties while proclaiming Christ with joy. His final video blogs and writings, filled with peace and purpose, still disciple people long after his death.[6]

The House Churches in Vietnam: Often overlooked, the underground church movement in Vietnam has endured severe crackdowns, with leaders imprisoned or exiled. And yet, it has grown from a few thousand to several million in the past few decades. Their faith thrives in the shadows.[7]

These are not superhumans. They're remnant leaders—scarred but steady, rejected yet radiant with Christ's presence.

WHEN YOU'RE RESISTED, YOU'RE IN GOOD COMPANY

Remnant renewal has always invited pushback. But you are not alone. Elijah thought he was the only one, but God had preserved seven thousand (1 Kgs 19:18). Jesus sent his disciples as sheep among wolves, but with the promise of his presence (Matt 10:16). Paul called Timothy to endure hardship as a good soldier of Christ (2 Tim 2:3), reminding him that suffering is part of the remnant's legacy.

Resistance doesn't mean you're wrong. Often, it means you're right where God wants you.

And here's the miracle: this resilient remnant doesn't end with you. It multiplies into others. The opposition you've endured becomes the soil for a new generation to grow. The tears you've cried water the seeds of next-generation leaders yet to rise.

As we turn the page to chapter 9, we discover that remnant leaders don't just survive resistance—they awaken the next generation through it. Keep reading.

Grace Will Lead Us Home.
6. Qureshi, *Seeking Allah, Finding Jesus*, for more of his story.
7. Church in Chains, "Vietnam."

REFLECTION AND RENEWAL

Scriptures for Meditation

- 1 Kgs 22:13–28—Micaiah's lone stand.
- Jer 20:7–11—The fire in his bones.
- Mark 6:1–6—Rejected in his hometown.
- 2 Cor 4:8–9—Pressed but not crushed.
- Rom 8:31–39—Nothing can separate us.
- 1 Pet 5:6–10—After you have suffered a little while.
- 2 Tim 1:6–14—Guarding the gift in suffering.
- Jas 1:2–4—Trials produce perseverance.
- Ps 46—God is our refuge.

Reflection Questions

1. Where have you experienced resistance, opposition, or discouragement in your call?
2. How have hardship or wounds shaped your leadership—for better or worse?
3. What habits or rhythms help you stay resilient in difficult seasons?
4. Who do you need beside you to keep going with strength and clarity?

Practice This Week

- Reflect: Where have you encountered the most resistance—in your soul, your setting, or your relationships? What has that resistance revealed about your foundation?

- Pray: Ask God to anchor your identity not in ministry success but in being his beloved. Write out Luke 3:22 and place it where you'll see it daily.
- Fast: Consider fasting one day this week from something that numbs your soul—news, social media, distractions. Use the space to listen, rest, and renew.
- Take a prayer walk and ask God to rekindle a specific area of calling that's grown dim under pressure.

CHAPTER 9

Awakening the Next-Generation Leader

IT STARTED WITH A SANDWICH—and a humorous insult.

Kevin Mahan, the campus pastor at LCBC Church in Manheim, Pennsylvania, and my good friend, had asked to meet for lunch. Over the past several years, we'd connected periodically over a meal together—sometimes he would ask me to mentor him, and sometimes I'd find myself learning just as much from him, especially about engaging the next generation in today's rapidly changing church landscape. He has a hunger to grow and a humble heart to match.

So there we were, seated at a local restaurant, diving into our lunches when Kevin leaned in and said, "The reason I wanted to meet today is because I'm about to turn forty, and I wanted to ask you what I'm in for in this next decade of my life—the forties . . . since, after all, you're much older than I am."

Ouch.

I laughed and told him that some things should never be said with your mouth full of chicken salad. We both cracked up, but I also knew this was a sacred moment. Underneath the humor was an invitation into deeper trust and investment. His ask honored me, not just because he was seeking advice but because he believed

I had something worth passing on. And it reminded me again of one of the most important callings on any remnant leader's life: mentoring and multiplying for the kingdom of God.

God isn't simply in the business of preserving faithful remnants; he multiplies them. And he does so through generational handoffs—like Elijah to Elisha, Moses to Joshua, Naomi to Ruth, and Paul to Timothy. The awakening of the next generation begins with relationships steeped in presence, trust, prayer, and purpose.

THE MAKING OF TIMOTHY

Before Timothy became Paul's protégé, before he was a key player in the early church's expansion, and long before he received those now-famous letters bearing his name, he was simply a young man with a unique legacy. Acts 16 introduces him as "the son of a Jewish woman who was a believer but whose father was a Greek" (v. 1). We later learn her name—Eunice—and his grandmother's name, Lois (2 Tim 1:5).

Their faith wasn't merely intellectual; it was embodied, lived out in the home. The Greek word used for "sincere faith" in Paul's letter (*anupokritos*) literally means "without hypocrisy."[1] That's the kind of faith within which Timothy was raised. His mother and grandmother didn't wait for a rabbi or a traveling preacher to disciple their boy. They did it themselves—with Scripture, with daily life, with love.

Then Paul entered the picture. When he returned to Lystra on his second missionary journey, he saw something in Timothy that was ready. Not finished. Not polished. But ready. And he invited Timothy to join the journey. He didn't start with a sermon or a leadership seminar. He started with a relationship. And over time, that relationship deepened into spiritual fatherhood.

Paul's mentorship wasn't just about tasks or ministry skills—it was rooted in calling. He reminded Timothy of his spiritual lineage, encouraged him to "fan into flame" the gift of God within

---

1. See ἀνυπόκριτος in Mounce, *Greek Grammar*, 78–79.

him (2 Tim 1:6), and even challenged him not to let others look down on his youth (1 Tim 4:12). Paul seemed to believe in the next generation before they believed in themselves.

SACRIFICE OR INVESTMENT?

Too often, older leaders frame their time with younger ones as a sacrifice: "I gave up my schedule to meet with them," or "I gave up my preferences so they could lead." But remnant leaders understand something deeper: this is not sacrifice—it's investment. And it's the kind of investment that carries exponential kingdom return.

Jesus didn't just heal the masses or preach to crowds; he poured deeply into a small group of followers who would become the foundation of the early church. He was intentional. Personal. Patient. And at times, even painfully honest. Discipleship is rarely clean—in fact, it's typically messy. But it's always catalytic when rooted in love.

If we want to see remnant renewal carry forward, we must not just *reach* the next generation—we must *raise* them. That means creating environments of formation and trust, recognizing emerging gifts, and letting them lead while they're still learning. Just as we did.

PROPHETIC VISION FOR WHAT COULD BE

Mentorship in the remnant is never about cloning—it's about calling forth what God has already placed within someone. I call it "treasure hunting"—going after the God-placed treasures that are embedded in a person's life, dusting them off, and putting them before the Lord to be refined and used for his glory. It's a prophetic act. Remnant leaders look beyond immaturity and inexperience to see a future God is already shaping.

Timothy wasn't perfect. He was timid. He struggled with confidence and stomach issues (1 Tim 5:23). And yet Paul called him "my true son in the faith" (1 Tim 1:2) and trusted him with complex pastoral tasks in places like Ephesus and Corinth.

This requires a different kind of vision—not reactive but redemptive. Not fixated on where someone is now but believing what they could become by the Spirit's power. When we mentor this way, we aren't just shaping people; we're partnering with the Spirit in shaping the future of the Jesus movement.

FORMATION SPACES THAT MULTIPLY

Remnant-minded churches, as well, foster leadership pipelines that grow from soil, not assembly lines. That's the difference. Leadership is formed in life-on-life spaces:

- Small groups where honest confession and spiritual accountability are practiced.
- Ministry huddles that include prayer, reflection, and real-life leadership "stretch assignments."
- Putting younger leaders into positions of authority, giving them tangible responsibilities—allowing them both to succeed and to fail, and then coaching them into greater fruit-bearing.
- Multi-generational relationships where younger leaders are not just seen but heard. "Don't let anyone look down on you because you are young, but set an example for the believers in speech, in conduct, in love, in faith and in purity," Paul told Timothy (1 Tim 4:12).

We're not talking about glamorous stages or platformed roles. We're talking about homes, lunch tables, coffee shops, mission sites. Every encounter becomes an altar for awakening. And they don't have to—and probably shouldn't—look like the "typical" settings.

REWILDING THE NEXT GENERATION: BEYOND THE USUAL PIPELINE

In fact, if the church is serious about awakening the next generation of leaders, it must stop waiting for them to come through the doors or climb predictable pipelines. Remnant leaders don't wait for the hungry to arrive—they go looking for them.

In a post-Christian, post-COVID, post-everything, deconstructed age, tomorrow's remnant leaders may not be found in today's seminary classrooms or youth group retreats (although clearly some are). They may be serving lattes in coffee shops, coding in co-working spaces, painting murals in underground venues, or organizing mutual aid on the streets.

Many of today's twenty- and thirty-somethings aren't necessarily drawn to platforms, programs, or polished professionalism. They seem to be allergic to performance-based faith, skeptical of institutionalism, and hungry for something that feels gritty, real, and costly. They don't necessarily want to lead the next church conference. Many want to follow Jesus in the dark alleys and broken systems of their cities.[2]

Remnant developers must learn to see potential apostolic fire behind cultural angst, prophetic vision beneath doubt, and spiritual hunger inside what some would label rebellion. Some of the most Spirit-sensitive, kingdom-ready young leaders don't look traditionally "churchy"—but their hearts are beating with God's dreams. I've had the privilege of engaging some of these leaders-in-the-making and am humbled by what they are embodying when it comes to the gospel. As mission strategist Alan Hirsch has argued, the church must recover an "incarnational impulse" to embed the gospel in the spaces where people already live, dream, and struggle.[3]

The task ahead isn't about tweaking old pipelines though—it's about *rewilding* leadership development altogether. The word *rewilding* evokes the process of returning something to its natural,

---

2. Barna, "CRC's Barna Describes Faith," for examples.
3. Hirsch, *Forgotten Ways*, 132.

untamed state.[4] The next generation doesn't need more polish—they need permission to burn with revival.

While remnant movements are Spirit-driven by nature and cannot be manufactured by humans, there are strategies for us present-day pastors and leaders to use in discerning what the Spirit may be birthing in the lives of those apostolic, prophetic, and spiritually hungry young people. These are not gimmicks. These are gospel-rooted strategies for cultivating Spirit-led leaders in the wild landscapes of a new era for the church. Here are four:

1. Look in the Margins, Not Just the Middle

As stated above, many catalytic young leaders will never show up through traditional church pathways. Some are bi-vocational dreamers, self-taught theologians, or digital content creators with massive influence but zero institutional recognition. Others are high schoolers organizing community gardens, college dropouts mentoring younger kids, or recovering addicts preaching on street corners.

These are not outliers—in today's culture, they are frontline missionaries (whether they realize it or not). In rare circumstances, they are "churched" in background—though they have disconnected from any formal faith community once out of high school. Many may be naïve or ignorant of any framework of a biblical *ecclesia* and may have no appreciation for doctrinal or denominational books of order—though their spirituality and praxis are palpable.

---

4. The term *rewilding* originates in ecological restoration, describing the process of returning landscapes to a more untamed, natural state by removing human control and reintroducing native species. See Monbiot, *Feral*. In Christian discipleship and mission, the metaphor has been surfacing as a way to describe returning to raw, Spirit-led expressions of faith outside institutional confines. See Scandrette, *Practicing the Way of Jesus*; Frost, *Road to Missional*; and Hirsch, *Forgotten Ways*. In my context, "rewilding" next-generation remnant leaders refers to the intentional recovery of missional instincts, spiritual courage, and creative faithfulness outside of institutional domestication (to play on the ecological term).

Jesus didn't recruit from the synagogue stage. He called disciples from fishing boats, tax booths, and revolutionary fringe groups. Likewise, remnant leaders must spot the shepherds among skateboarders, the prophets in downtown city studio apartments, and the apostolic builders who've never cracked open a theology textbook.[5]

I wonder what we would learn if we equipped our leaders and church members to form listening posts in our communities—literally or metaphorically speaking. What if we would send trusted leaders into spaces the congregation rarely shows up—tattoo parlors, refugee communities, ethnic communities that reflect an ethos different than our own, art shows, mall food courts—and commission those leaders not to lead with answers but simply to build relationships and listen for the Spirit's direction?

If those spaces are too risky for us, or perhaps they don't define our suburban or agricultural milieu, then perhaps we stake out the margins within our communities—the ones that we do know about, yet do not attend to. I've encountered many young leaders-in-the-making that are hair stylists, restaurant servers, musicians, fitness instructors, or bartenders. We may discover next-generation leaders that are hidden within our own backyards.

I have an ongoing leadership principle that says, "Don't ask the congregation to do anything that I'm not willing to do first." If that's true for you, then being a leader may mean you will need to take the first step in living into this mission.

2. Embrace Decentralized Discipleship and Digital Mission

Whether or not we realize it, the next generation is being spiritually formed more by podcasts, TikTok, and YouTube than by pulpits or Sunday school.[6] While this raises valid concerns, it

---

5. In addition to Hirsch, check out Frost, *Road to Missional* and Claiborne, *Irresistible Revolution*.

6. Im, *You Are What You Do*. Daniel frames an interesting perspective on this digital reality.

also creates fresh opportunities. COVID-19 propelled the leaders in my church to create an online presence earlier than originally planned. Post-pandemic, many churches wondered when to disconnect in order to go back into traditional pathways for worship and discipleship—i.e., "Get their butts back into the pews, Pastor!" Our leaders, however, decided to expand our digital outreach—anticipating this generational trend and its implications.

Micro-learning models, peer-led Discovery Bible Groups over Signal or WhatsApp, and coaching through group chats are already discipling thousands worldwide.[7]

Remnant leaders must embrace decentralized, mobile, and reproducible methods of equipping—training leaders in living rooms, voice notes, and short-form media with deep biblical substance. It's crazy, I know. We are facing a "wild" ride in transitioning from "the way we've always done it." Yet, it's hard to disciple a next generation if they're not coming.

So, what do we do? First, if we haven't already done so, we need to learn the language of the digital world—like the difference between Instagram and TikTok, for example. While we may not need to be fluent, we need to know at least some of the basics to communicate with the next generation who grew up with the world in their back pocket. Every Monday, my worship and tech team (all in their twenties and thirties) meets to plan and implement what goes out into the social media world based on our Sunday's worship. Throughout the week, the team is posting highlights, reels, shorts, and invitations. We must be intentional in learning the language of our mission field.

Second, I wonder what it would be like for our congregations to launch "field-based apprenticeships" where discipleship happens in real time—through missional experiments, shared meals, spiritual rhythms, and risk-taking obedience, equipping younger leaders to engage the younger generations within their spheres of influence. We can't wait for people to enroll in a program; we need to bring formation into the flow of their actual lives—an embedded discipleship process.

---

7. International Project, "Philosophy of Ministry."

3. Reimagine Mentorship as Co-Discovery

In a culture overwhelmed by content, clarity of calling matters more than clarity of doctrine—at least in the early stages of development. Many potential remnant leaders have fire in their souls but no formal training yet. They are not theologically immature as much as theologically in process—naming injustice, longing for purpose, and yearning for a life that costs something.

We must not quench that flame by insisting they align with every nuance of denominational orthodoxy from day one. Instead, we have an opportunity to disciple them in real life and let doctrine mature as it marinates in the field.[8]

Postmodern leaders often reject hierarchy but deeply crave authenticity. They don't want a "sage on a stage" (so I've been told)—they want a friend on the journey. Remnant leadership development must move from top-down transmission to relational co-discovery. We don't hand young leaders a manual and say, "Do this." We invite them to wrestle with Scripture in community, listen to God together, and live the questions they're carrying.

In recent years, I've tried to be intentional in doing two things with people we hire for our church staff: First, hire younger, gifted leaders who are solid in character, creative and innovative in their field of hire, and not afraid to take risks for the sake of the gospel. And second, when presented with a challenge or dilemma, ask them much more frequently, "What would *you* do?" rather than me providing potential solutions.

What I've discovered is that their solutions many times blow mine out of the water. Sure, they may need some guidance in relational dynamics or providing leadership when most of their volunteers are two and three times their age—but that's our job as patient, seasoned leaders, right?

---

8. Hirsch and Frost, *Shaping of Things*, 56–59. Hirsch and Frost argue that belonging often precedes believing in postmodern mission.

As Dallas Willard once wrote, true spiritual formation is not about information alone—it's about a "curriculum for Christlikeness."[9]

So, how about if we cultivate coaching relationships built on trust, mutual learning, and mission. Let's train seasoned leaders to guide by listening, to model more than instruct, and to walk alongside instead of above—giving the next generation genuinely significant roles of leadership and seeing what they do with them.

4. Name the Hidden Giftings Others Miss

Many emerging leaders carry a calling that doesn't fit into clean categories. They might not preach, lead worship, or run a ministry team—but they carry prophetic imagination, catalytic hospitality, or a burden for justice that refuses to quit. These callings often get overlooked in churches—or by churches—that prioritize stage presence or institutional roles.

Remnant leaders must become experts in *naming* what God has deposited in people, when it doesn't look "churchy." Jesus saw a rock in Peter and a missionary in a persecutor (Paul), and Paul saw a preacher in a teenager (Timothy). We must do the same.

Next-gen remnant leaders are especially attuned to the overlooked. They recognize gifting in those shaped by artistic instinct, justice-driven activism, apostolic risk-taking, or neurodivergent brilliance. They are uniquely gifted—and they're watching to see if the church has room for what God has placed in them. Many do not feel welcomed.

Some express deep spiritual insight through painting, photography, or songwriting—artists who prophetically image heaven through beauty. Others channel holy fire into justice advocacy—fighting trafficking, reforming prison systems, or standing with the marginalized. Still others have entrepreneurial instincts—apostolically starting networks, microchurches, or nonprofits without waiting for permission. And many—especially those who

---

9. Willard, *Divine Conspiracy*, 276.

are neurodivergent—bring intense focus, original thinking, and spiritual sensitivity that doesn't always show up in traditional environments but reveals profound kingdom impact when nurtured.[10]

In 1 Cor 12, Paul reminds us that the Spirit distributes gifts "just as he determines" (v. 11), and that the parts of the body that seem weaker or less visible are actually *indispensable*. Next-gen remnant leaders embody that truth by identifying and honoring the gifts others overlook. These leaders aren't "outside the mold"— they are the *new* mold God is shaping for the church's future. The task is not to fix them but to see them, to hear them, to equip them, and to *free* them.

Hear me: I'm no expert in these terrains—but I'm trying. I'm intentionally stretching myself to see and to live outside of my comfort zones. Once, I was one of those young people trying to find my voice and my place in a call that originally didn't make sense to me. I thank God for those prior generation representatives who gave me opportunities to lead, space to fail, and the mentoring I needed to both temper and channel my wild but emerging leadership gifts.

I want to be that kind of representative for the next generation. Do you? The remnant is counting on us to invest in them what others had invested in us.

THE BOLD FUTURE OF REMNANT LEADERSHIP

So, if we keep looking for leaders in sanitized spaces with safe résumés, we may miss the ones God is already anointing. The next generation of remnant leaders may be raw, gritty, poetic, entrepreneurial, and possibly even scarred.[11] They won't necessarily fit the mold—but neither did David, Esther, Peter, or Mary Magdalene.

Remnant renewal doesn't begin with credentials. It begins with courage. The church must release young leaders into the

---

10. For some interesting reading on these examples, see Fujimura, *Art and Faith*; Hardwick, *Disability and the Church*; Claiborne, *Irresistible Revolution*; and Hirsch and Catchim, *Permanent Revolution*.

11. Nouwen, *Wounded Healer*, 82–83.

wild—not unformed but unafraid. We need to train them to hear God, walk humbly, and take risks—then let theology catch up as they move. With the Spirit as their guide, the church as their tribe, mentors by their side, and the kingdom of God as their ride, they will carry awakening into places we've long abandoned.

MODERN THREADS OF MULTIPLICATION

This pursuit of the next generation is not optional anymore—it's prophetic. Around the world, we are witnessing modern movements of renewal being led by the very kinds of hidden leaders the world has overlooked—examples of which we have seen throughout this book. From Filipino marketplace catalysts to digital missionaries in closed countries, a new remnant is already rising.

Equipping young people to engage the remnant rewilding process gives us an opportunity to partner with the Spirit in multiplying the Jesus movement and awakening God's church. Consider these examples:

The Passion Conference and Louie Giglio's Vision

In the late 1990s, Louie Giglio began hosting gatherings for college students under the banner of "Passion." He saw not just a generation needing Jesus but a generation called to global purpose in Jesus. Today, Passion has catalyzed a wave of young leaders across the world—mobilizing them toward worship, justice, and local church impact.[12]

Young Leaders at Exponential and the Future Church

At the annual Exponential Conference, young church planters and next-gen leaders aren't just attending—they're speaking, leading, and innovating.[13] Networks like the SEND Institute and Church

12. Giglio, *Comeback*, 152–54.
13. For example, see https://exponential.org.

Multiplication Collective intentionally equip younger leaders for missional impact, trusting them with real responsibility while surrounding them with mentors. I so wish this was available when I was just starting out in ministry!

Intergenerational Discipleship Through Christian Endeavor

In countless churches, small shifts are yielding huge fruit: older members opening their homes, young adults co-leading groups, churches hiring full-time "leadership development" staff. My good friend Dave Coryell has harnessed this energy in an exponential way. He is the global director at Christian Endeavor—a worldwide and interdenominational movement that is equipping young people to live Christ-centered lives.[14] CE focuses on developing youth into leaders for God's kingdom agenda by providing resources to local churches, youth pastors, senior pastors, and congregations that multiply the gospel's impact. In his recently published book—*Less Like Hippos . . . More Like Honey Bees: Reject Consumerism, Embrace Maturity, Change How the World Does Youth Ministry*—Dave explores three pivotal strategies for mentorship: championing, empowering, and motivating youth. These aren't flashy strategies. They're faithful ones. I've mentored Dave for thirty years. Dave now mentors *thousands*—directly and through others—throughout the world. The remnant is multiplying.

A KINGDOM CHAIN REACTION

You never know what's being set in motion over a sandwich. That day with my friend Kevin reminded me that mentoring the next generation is less about having all the answers and more about showing up with presence, perspective, and permission. When we open space for younger leaders to ask, wrestle, grow, and lead, we awaken them to their mission mandate.

---

14. Christian Endeavor, "About Christian Endeavor."

And if we're lucky, they might even return the favor and mentor us as well.

This is exactly why I have sought out opportunities to engage younger leaders within the local churches to which I've been appointed. It's also why I love working with students at Kairos University as an affiliate professor and faculty mentor. Kairos is built on a foundation of mentoring and multiplying for the sake of the kingdom. The "classroom" is the student's vocational context. The "faculty"—while inclusive of traditional professors—consists of a team of mentors committed to equipping the student not simply for a degree but for advancing the kingdom of God.

The remnant multiplies—not just through revival meetings or church strategies but through lives poured out in quiet faithfulness into the next generation right where they are.

In the next chapter, we'll look at how remnant leaders don't just birth new things; they revive what others have abandoned—bringing life to forgotten callings, discarded places, and people the world has written off.

REFLECTION AND RENEWAL

Scriptures for Meditation

2 Tim 1:5–7—"I am reminded of your sincere faith."

1 Thess 2:8—"Because we loved you so much . . ."

Ps 145:4—"One generation commends your works to another."

1 Tim 4:12—"Don't let anyone look down on you because you are young."

Reflection Questions

1. Who were the spiritual mothers, fathers, or mentors who saw something in you when others didn't? How did they awaken your faith or calling?

2. Are you currently investing in a younger leader or potential disciple? If not, what's holding you back?

3. What generational assumptions do you need to lay down in order to listen more deeply to what God is doing in younger lives today?

4. How might you create more space—relational, spiritual, missional, and in leadership—for the next generation to risk, grow, and lead?

5. In your current ministry or church context, where are the next-generation leaders waiting to be seen, trusted, and empowered?

Practice This Week

- *Name and Notice*: Ask the Holy Spirit to highlight one younger person (or emerging leader) around you. Pray for them daily this week and intentionally affirm something you see in them.

- *Initiate a Conversation*: Reach out and invite a younger person to coffee or a walk (utilizing, of course, appropriate boundaries consistent with age and gender). Ask them about their hopes, struggles, and dreams. Just listen—and let it be the start of a mentoring relationship, not a one-time talk.

- *Create a Small On-Ramp*: Give a younger person a safe opportunity to lead something small—whether it's part of a meeting, prayer, service opportunity, or creative idea. Debrief with them afterward and encourage reflection.

- *Tell Your Story*: Share a short version of how God has led you and what you've learned in the process. Frame it not as advice but as wisdom earned—and leave space for questions and dialogue.

- *Fast from Control*: In one leadership moment this week, intentionally step back and let someone younger lead—even if it's messier. Ask God to grow your trust in his work in them.

CHAPTER 10

How Remnant Leaders Revive What Others Have Abandoned

As I write this chapter, I'm attending my denomination's regional annual conference. Once a year, clergy and laity from across the region gather to worship, learn, discern direction, and wrestle with the challenges of equipping our congregations to make disciples in today's world.

This afternoon's session included the annual memorial service. We read the names of clergy and clergy spouses who passed away over the last year. With each name spoken, family members and friends were invited to stand. A moment of silence followed. Then an ancient bell tolled, and the next name was called.

I stood from the first name to the last—not because I knew every person but because I wanted to honor the cumulative offering of their lives. Their ministries, prayers, sacrifices, and sermons helped shape the body of Christ that now shapes me. As the bell echoed through the room, I was overcome with gratitude—for the legacy of faith they left behind and for the gospel that moved through their lives into others.

Then came another list.

Names of churches.

Congregations that had closed their doors in the past year due to decline or financial strain. After each name, the bell tolled again. But this time, the sound felt different. Heavier. These churches represented entire histories of transformation: baptisms, weddings, hospital visits, food pantries, Christmas Eve services, children's choirs, community prayers. Their stories weren't just spiritual—they were deeply local. Deeply human.

And yet, their endings were marked only by silence, and then a bell.

I found myself standing again—this time with a different kind of ache. I understand that some churches finish their life cycle. Not all are meant to live forever. But I couldn't shake the sense that something sacred was being lost without being reimagined. There was no vision of resurrection. No plan for rebirth. No transition of kingdom presence into the communities those churches once served. At least none that I heard or saw. Yet.

Remnant leaders ask a different kind of question:

- What about the people still living in those neighborhoods—who still need to encounter the love of Christ?
- What happens to the witness of the gospel in places where the light once burned but now seems to have flickered out?

In God's kingdom economy, God redeems not just souls—but streets, communities, and everything we too quickly call dead.

And this isn't a new idea.

It's the kind of story we've seen before—in a valley of dry bones, handed to a prophet with barely enough hope to whisper the word *life*.

DRY BONES AND A PROPHETIC ASSIGNMENT

Ezekiel 37 is one of the most iconic images of restoration in the Bible. But to feel its weight, we must enter the mosaic moment—not as spectators but as prophets. Ezekiel is taken "by the Spirit" to a valley of dry bones, not merely dead bodies but *long*-dead, dismembered, and scattered bodies (vv. 1–2). The Hebrew phrase for "very dry" (*yeveshot me'od*) paints the picture of utter lifelessness—hope buried under centuries of ruin.[1]

Then God asks Ezekiel a loaded question, "Son of man, can these bones live?" (v. 3). What a profound question—one that goes against any common human sense! Notice Ezekiel's cautious answer: "Sovereign Lord, you alone know." The Lord then downloads a rather strange request for the prophet: "Prophesy to these bones and say to them, 'Dry bones, hear the word of the Lord!'" (v. 4)—a phrase uttered under the breath by many pastors of seemingly lifeless congregations prior to getting up to preach!

God announces that he's going to breathe new life into those bones, put flesh on them, and by doing so, they "will know that I am the Lord" (v. 6). God is about to raise up—literally—a remnant, prophetically formed out of that which looks utterly lifeless.

Ezekiel doesn't presume that God is about to do a miracle, but he doesn't deny the possibility either. And that's where every remnant leader stands—in that tension between reality and promise. God still has a plan for Judah and Jerusalem—but that plan needs a faithful remnant to carry it out. One that God himself will raise up.

Notice that God commands Ezekiel not to fix the bones but to prophesy to them. Revival begins not with renovation but with the word of the Lord. As Ezekiel speaks, bone connects to bone, sinew grows, and breath enters the reformed bodies (vv. 7–10). What was once scattered becomes nothing shy of a massive incarnational interventional plan—and a prophetic object lesson for Ezekiel: "Son of man, these bones are the people of Israel. They say, 'Our bones are dried up and our hope is gone; we are cut off'" (v. 11). The people do not see hope, but God is the Author of life and hope. God has the ability to raise the dead, to make all things new.

---

1. Block, *Book of Ezekiel*, 379. The phrase "very dry" in Ezek 37:2 comes from the Hebrew *yeveshot me'od*, where *yeveshot* denotes dryness or withering, and *me'od* intensifies it to mean "exceedingly" or "utterly," implying complete hopelessness.

This passage reminds us that God's resurrection power isn't just spiritual—it's structural as well. He reassembles what is disconnected. He restores the sinews of worship, mission, and community in places where they've been lost.

NEW WINE, NEW WINESKINS

In the New Testament, Jesus warns, "No one pours new wine into old wineskins. Otherwise, the wine will burst the skins. . . . No, they pour new wine into new wineskins" (Mark 2:22). In context, Jesus is addressing the inability of the old religious systems to contain the vitality of the kingdom he is inaugurating. But Jesus' words also echo forward into every generation.

Abandonment often occurs when the vessel can no longer carry the mission. But remnant leaders are those who see not just the decay of old structures—but the possibility of reformation, or more specifically, resurrection. New wine requires pliability. Remnant leaders do not merely replicate past models—they allow the Spirit to reshape the container.

And often, it means starting with what others have discarded.

THE REMNANT AS RESTORERS

Remnant leaders are not merely survivors of spiritual drought—they are restorers with sacred imagination. Their role is both prophetic and quite often parabolic. Like Nehemiah inspecting the ruins of Jerusalem by night, they do not turn away from brokenness but move toward it with burden and hope. Restoration and revival are not nostalgia; they are Spirit-filled acts of reclaiming what God originally intended.

In Neh 3, the Hebrew word for "repair" (*chazaq*) implies both strengthening and encouragement. In Isa 58:12 as well, God calls his people "repairers of broken walls" and "restorers of streets with dwellings." Ezekiel's vision of the valley of dry bones is a prophetic blueprint for remnant-based revival. The Hebrew word for "breath" (*ruach*) is the same word used for "Spirit" and "wind" (Ezek 37:9), signaling that divine revival is not mechanical but Spirit-inspired. The bones did not come alive because of Ezekiel's strategy but because of God's sovereign word and breath.[2]

The remnant is not merely the leftovers of spiritual decline but the seedbed of divine renewal. There is intentionality to the remnant rather than passivity. The remnant steps into abandoned places—whether in the city, the church, or the human heart—and strengthens what remains with truth, compassion, and holy grit. They are not afraid to get their hands dirty because they believe no place—and no person—is too far gone when God breathes on it. To revive is to look at the rubble and still declare, "This can live again."

HOW REMNANT LEADERS REVIVE AND REIMAGINE

In Matthew's Gospel, Jesus tells a parable: "The kingdom of heaven is like treasure hidden in a field" (Matt 13:44). Modern people (like us) scope out community yard sales to find "trash to treasure" deals. Kingdom leaders, especially remnant ones, are treasure hunters scoping out overlooked places and people. But how do they revive what others have abandoned? Here are a few strategies:

1. They Recognize What Others No Longer See

Remnant leaders walk into decline and see dormant potential. They hear echoes of former glory but listen deeper for the Spirit's whisper of future promise. Like Nehemiah surveying Jerusalem's ruins by night, they grieve—but they also plan.

Remnant leaders make a habit of revisiting abandoned callings and anointings as well—not only in places but in people too. Many lives are littered with unfulfilled assignments and dusty dreams—things God spoke long ago that were never acted upon

---

2. See Block, *Book of Ezekiel*, 379–85, for a broader context and explanation.

or were shelved after pain or resistance. Remnant leaders are often directed to revisit these abandoned callings, to give credential to what God had set in motion once before. They help people recover the voice of God they once heard but now doubt, or once denied but now have heard.

Like Paul reminding Timothy to "fan into flame the gift of God" (2 Tim 1:6), these leaders call forth dormant gifts with tenderness and courage. They ask questions like, "What did God once say that you've since buried?" and "What if that call is still alive?" Revival begins when forgotten anointings are reawakened and reactivated, when that which is hidden is revealed and inspired.

2. They Find Treasure in What Others Overlook or Throw Away

Remnant leaders see value where others see waste. They carry the perspective of Jesus who called fishermen, tax collectors, and zealots—not likely candidates for world-changing discipleship from a first-century human perspective. To the watching world, the overlooked are often liabilities, but to the remnant, they may be kingdom assets.

Isaiah 45:3 speaks of "treasures hidden in darkness"—people and places where redemptive gold lies beneath layers of failure or obscurity. Remnant leaders dig with grace and discernment, believing that the people most broken may carry the greatest potential for beauty. They don't just believe in second chances; they expect God to show up in the impossible.

In abandoned churches or neighborhoods, as with people, the story is usually one of decline or depression. But remnant leaders reframe it and reclaim it as holy ground. Loss becomes compost for resurrection. They don't ask, "How do we fix this?" but rather, "What could God do here if we said yes?'

3. They Repurpose Ruins for Fresh Mission

In Isa 61:4, God promises that the restored will become rebuilders: "They will rebuild the ancient ruins and restore the places long devastated." Remnant leaders don't throw out what's old necessarily; they reimagine it with the Spirit's vision. An aging church building becomes a refuge for recovering addicts. An old liturgy becomes a new path for spiritual depth. A scarred community becomes fertile soil for justice and discipleship. These leaders have the creativity of kingdom entrepreneurs and the hearts of shepherds. They don't see ruins as liabilities—they see foundations for something redemptive and new.

Yes, Jesus compares the kingdom to treasure hidden in a field (Matt 13:44). Often, the most overlooked people carry the greatest potential, yet they remain hidden behind old structures and infrastructures. Remnant leaders learn to look not at outward appearances but at kingdom potential. But here's the deal: we don't see if we don't look; and we don't look if we're not praying for what God wants to do.

4. They Reframe Failure Through the Lens of Redemption

Where others see the end, the remnant sees the middle. They are fluent in God's paradoxical language of reversal—where shame becomes testimony and loss becomes seed. Jesus did this when he showed his scars after resurrection. Paul reframed his imprisonment as a platform for gospel advancement. God tells Ezekiel to prophesy twice: first to the bones, then to the breath. There is formation, then filling. Remnant leaders disciple others through this same pattern—calling forth structure (formation) and waiting for Spirit empowerment (filling).

In doing so, remnant leaders learn to tell stories differently—not by denying pain but by refusing to let pain have the last word. They teach others to reinterpret failure, not as disqualification but as divine preparation. This reframing is not spin; it is a faith-saturated perspective that holds fast to Rom 8:28—"And we know that in all things God works for the good of those who love him, who have been called according to his purpose"—even when things still look like death. I envision this model of remnant renewal as similar to church planting, but in harvest-to-be soil that has been lying fallow to restore its fertility.

MODERN THREADS OF RENEWAL

The work of the remnant is not just an ancient pattern though—it's alive today. Across generations and global movements, we continue to see God stirring renewal through unexpected people in forgotten places. What once seemed abandoned is being repurposed. What was broken is becoming beautiful. From underground churches in restricted nations to creative communities in post-Christian cities, the Spirit is still breathing on dry bones. These modern threads of renewal remind us that the remnant is not rare—it's just often hidden, waiting to be awakened and released for such a time as this. Consider these few examples:

Tennessee Valley Church Revitalization: A dying church of twelve in rural Tennessee began praying and visiting homes. Within three years, it became a bilingual, multi-generational church—pastored by a formerly homeless man discipled by an elder.[3]

Portland's Church-to-Coffeehouse Transformation: A disbanded church sold its building to a mission-minded group who transformed it into a missional café, art space, and home for worship gatherings. Today, it draws seekers through hospitality and justice partnerships.[4]

Urban Neighborhood Resurrection: In cities all over America, faith-based organizations and architectural firms, as well as local congregations, have reclaimed church buildings and repurposed

---

3. Beck, *Deep Roots, Wild Branches*, 93–94.
4. See Crisp, "Bell Tower Coffee."

them as after-school centers, worship spaces, low-income housing, and community kitchens—prioritizing presence over platform.[5]

A DEEPER FIRE

Reviving what others have abandoned is not for the faint of heart. It demands more than vision—it requires endurance. Remnant leaders don't just see potential in forgotten places; they keep showing up when progress is slow, when applause is absent, and when the cost feels high. They live by a deeper fire. In the world's eyes, their work may seem hidden or unfinished. But in God's eyes, their faithfulness is fruit. And it's precisely that kind of perseverance—quiet, steady, and often unseen—that carries the embers of true awakening.

In chapter 11, we'll explore what it takes to stay steady when no one's clapping—and how remnant leaders learn to lead not for recognition but from the presence of God. We open with the story of Jeremiah—but not just in the obvious way. His backstory tells even more.

REFLECTION AND RENEWAL

Scriptures for Meditation

Ezek 37:1–14—The valley of dry bones.

Lam 3:21–24—Hope in the middle of suffering.

Matt 13:44–46—Discovering hidden treasure in unexpected places.

Mark 2:21–22—The call to prepare new wineskins for kingdom movement.

Rom 4:18–21—Abraham's hope against hope.

2 Cor 4:7–9—God's treasure in jars of clay.

---

5. For one example organization, see https://www.bricksandmortals.org.

2 Cor 4:16-18—Fixing our eyes on the unseen.

Reflection Questions

1. Where in your life or community do you see "dry bones" that God may want to revive? What "dry bones" situations have you given up on? What might God be calling you to speak into again?
2. Have you ever given up on someone or something too quickly? What would it mean to revisit that space with fresh faith?
3. Are you clinging to an old "wineskin"? What would releasing it make room for?
4. Who around you might be a "hidden treasure" God wants to unearth?
5. Where is your voice needed right now—to speak God's word into weary people?

Practice This Week

- Walk your neighborhood slowly and prayerfully. Ask God to show you what's been abandoned, overlooked, or dismissed—and to help you see it through his eyes.
- Visit a place that feels "dry" in your life—whether physical (an old ministry site), relational (an estranged connection), or spiritual (a weary practice). Sit in it, pray over it, and ask God to speak to you through it.
- Write a hope declaration over a current valley. Speak it out loud each day this week.
- Encourage someone who's ready to quit. Be their Ezekiel. Speak breath into their bones.

CHAPTER 11

Staying Steady When No One's Clapping

IN AN AGE OF performance, the Hebrew prophet Jeremiah's story reminds us of what it means to remain faithful when no one notices—or worse, when they reject you. Called as a youth and commissioned to uproot and rebuild, Jeremiah's ministry spanned four decades of resistance, rebellion, and exile (Jer 1:4–10). He preached unpopular truth. He warned of judgment. He was imprisoned, mocked, and even thrown into a cistern (Jer 38:6). He watched the collapse of Jerusalem, the desecration of the temple, and the shattering of national hopes.[1]

And still, he persevered in his mission.

What makes Jeremiah especially important for remnant leaders is that he remained faithful not because of results but because of revelation. God had called him—and that was enough. It had to be. Even when Jerusalem fell and exile began, Jeremiah stayed rooted to his commission. He bought a field while the city burned (Jer 32:9–15)—a prophetic act that declared "God is not done here." He spoke hope into desolation, penning promises of a new covenant even while sitting in the rubble (Jer 31:31–34).

---

1. See Woolverton, *Prophet and Loss*, 17–47, for more of my reflections on Jeremiah.

Indeed, Jeremiah teaches us that being part of the remnant doesn't mean popularity or power—it means perseverance. Long-suffering. Endurance. Remaining faithful to the Lord's call to the end.

Jeremiah exemplifies the remnant heart: someone who remains rooted in God's voice when everything else is falling apart. His faithfulness wasn't measured in visible fruit but in unshakable obedience. When others chased security, Jeremiah chose surrender. When others sought status, Jeremiah stayed with the rubble.

This is the unattended work of remnant leaders: to remain in hidden places, to nurture life in barren soil, and to listen for God when the crowd has gone silent. *We must remember our call.*

But there are backstories to Jeremiah's quest—stories of hidden figures that embody the call of the remnant: Baruch, Jeremiah's scribe; and Uriah, Jeremiah's contemporary. Both stories display the good and the evil of humanity.

IN THE SHADOW OF THE PROPHET

Sometimes I imagine what it was like for Baruch to sit in the shadows, ink-stained hands cramping as he scratched down Jeremiah's words of judgment and hope. There were no crowds gathering to thank him. No promise of a book deal. No publisher's advance. No book launch. Only a weary prophet, burdened by the word of the Lord, pacing in a room that smelled of dust and sweat, dictating warnings to him that no one wanted to hear.

Baruch, the son of Neriah, was a scribe—a position of some standing in the royal courts (Jer 36:4). He could have used his skills for more pleasant work, I'm sure, maybe drafting diplomatic letters or chronicling royal history. Instead, he aligned himself with a rejected prophet whose message had been ridiculed and whose life was under constant threat. More than once, Baruch put himself at risk by simply writing down what God had told Jeremiah to say.

In one dramatic moment, Jeremiah is in hiding, unable to deliver his message to the people himself. So, he tells Baruch, "I am restricted; I am not allowed to go to the LORD's temple. So you go to the house of the LORD on a day of fasting and read to the people from the scroll the words of the LORD" (Jer 36:5-6). Baruch obeys. He stands in the temple courts and reads words that will surely make the ruling class angry. And they do. The scroll is eventually brought to King Jehoiakim, who casually cuts it up and burns it piece by piece (Jer 36:23).

How do you keep showing up when your work goes up in flames?

Baruch must have wrestled with disillusionment. I would have. At one point, the Lord gives him a personal message through Jeremiah—one that acknowledges Baruch's inner turmoil: "You said, 'Woe to me! The LORD has added sorrow to my pain; I am worn out with groaning and find no rest'" (Jer 45:3). God sees him. And God doesn't rebuke him for being weary. Instead, he gives Baruch a gentle reframing: "Should you then seek great things for yourself? Do not seek them" (Jer 45:5). In other words, "You're not invisible to me. But you must decide whether your reward is recognition—or obedience."

A HIDDEN PROPHET

And then there's Uriah—not the husband of Bathsheba, a different Uriah (or Urijah, depending on your translation). Most have never heard of him. Until recently, I didn't really either—or rather, I had read about him, but I didn't pay much attention to his story. He's mentioned in just four verses—Jer 26:20-23.

Now his story unnerves me.

Uriah was a prophet during the same time as Jeremiah. Like Jeremiah, he prophesied against Jerusalem and Judah in the name of the Lord. Like Jeremiah, his words angered King Jehoiakim. But unlike Jeremiah, apparently Uriah had no protector. He fled to Egypt in fear, but Jehoiakim hunted him down, dragged him back, and had him executed. His body was thrown into a common grave (v. 23).

No applause. No rescue. No vindication in his lifetime. Just quiet obedience, then silence.

And yet—his name is preserved in Scripture, woven into Jeremiah's story not as a footnote (although some translations put these verses within parentheses) but as a reminder that prophetic faithfulness doesn't always get a happy ending. Sometimes it gets a shallow grave. Sometimes the reward for long-haul obedience is simply being known by God and remembered in eternity.

STANDING IN THE RUINS

These men—Baruch the scribe, Uriah the slain prophet, and Jeremiah of course—embody what it means to stay steady when no one is clapping. They didn't see revival in their day. They saw resistance. Rejection. Grief. But they kept saying yes to God.

Remnant leaders don't always stand on stages. Sometimes they stand in ruins, holding a pen or a message that no one wants. They remain faithful in anonymity, trusting that the God who called them sees what no one else does.

Their faithfulness challenges today's remnant leaders to redefine fruitfulness—not in terms of applause or platform but in terms of obedience over time. In quiet perseverance. In long, slow, unseen faithfulness. Because sometimes the most powerful ministry isn't found in the spotlight but in the shadows—where the Spirit sees, even if no one else does.

That's why remnant leaders must learn the discipline of staying when it would be easier to quit.

Difficult, for sure. I've been there. Maybe you have too.

Maybe that's where you're at right now.

If it is, then I want to encourage you—indeed, *challenge* you—to remember your call!

Revival doesn't always come in the time—or the way—we expect. The results we long for may not unfold during our tenure. However, our call is not to manufacture fruit—but to abide long enough for roots to deepen, even through the bitterness of winter or the droughts of summer. Obedience is our call. However, the fruit of our labor is in God's hands.

As Walter Brueggemann reminds us in reference to Jeremiah, "Jeremiah's vocation was to live between the end of one world and the beginning of another."[2] Remnant leaders today do the same. They live in the "already, but not yet"—trusting that God is still at work even in seasons of apparent abandonment.

FAITHFUL FINISHERS AND THE LONG OBEDIENCE

As with Jeremiah, we find a pattern throughout Scripture: God's most enduring work often comes through people who finish well when no one's cheering. A few more examples:

- Anna the prophetess worshiped faithfully in the temple for decades before she saw the Messiah (Luke 2:36–38).

- Caleb, at age eighty-five, still believed the promise of God and asked for the mountain he was once promised (Josh 14:10–12).

- Paul, writing in prison near the end of his life, said with humble clarity, "I have fought the good fight, I have finished the race, I have kept the faith" (2 Tim 4:7).

- Moses, though barred from the promised land, led with faith until his final breath and passed the mantle to Joshua with courage and clarity (Deut 34:5–9). His finish wasn't about personal success but about ensuring the next generation carried the mission forward.

- Barzillai, an elderly supporter of King David, quietly showed loyal love and sacrificial hospitality during David's exile, refusing accolades in his old age while advocating for a younger servant instead (2 Sam 19:31–39). His quiet faithfulness shows how finishing well doesn't always look like leading from the front.

---

2. Brueggemann, *Hopeful Imagination*, 1.

- John, the beloved disciple, finished his life in exile on Patmos yet remained a vessel of revelation and vision when most had forgotten him (Rev 1:9-10). Isolated and aged, he still received and recorded the final word of God's redemptive plan.

These weren't headline-makers. They were faithful finishers. They burned with a steady fire long after others had cooled. These finishers didn't cling to spotlight or status. They endured through pain, obscurity, and age with a faith sharpened by time.

Remnant leaders aren't measured by quick results but by long obedience.[3] In a culture obsessed with rapid influence, they remain rooted in God's presence, even when no one's clapping. Remnant leaders learn to cultivate the inner life that can carry the weight of longevity—not just starting well but enduring with grace.

FAITHFUL FINISHERS KEEP SHOWING UP

The least celebrated spiritual gift in the remnant might be endurance. Our world applauds platforms, charisma, and viral moments. But the kingdom honors those who keep showing up—especially when no one else does. Hebrews 10:36 reminds us, "You need to persevere so that when you have done the will of God, you will receive what he has promised."

In a remnant age, leadership often happens under the radar. The fruit may come later, but faithfulness starts now.

RECOGNIZING THE SIGNS OF NEW LIFE

Remnant leaders, therefore, must develop resurrection eyesight. Like Jeremiah buying a field or Anna recognizing the Messiah in a baby, they discern signs of new life when others see only decay or insignificance.

One of the deepest lessons of the remnant is this: don't miss the mustard seed moments. The kingdom grows underground before it sprouts in public. You might see those seeds in a prodigal

---

3. Peterson, *Long Obedience*, for a great read on this topic.

showing curiosity again, a young believer asking deeper questions, a leader recommitting to prayer. Here are a few other signs to look for:

1. Hunger for the Word—Not Just Information but Transformation

When people begin to crave Scripture with fresh eyes and open hearts, it's a sign the Spirit is stirring. It's not about more Bible studies for study's sake but an awakening to God's voice that changes how people live, serve, and love.[4]

2. Deepening Prayer—Especially Among the Overlooked

When prayer isn't just a pre-meeting, pre-dinner formality but becomes a desperate, daily lifeline for people—especially those who used to stay quiet—it signals spiritual renewal. Often, it's the prayer meetings no one notices that become the womb of revival.

3. Reconciliation and Repentance—Relationships Begin to Heal

The gospel always leads to new life—across family rifts, racial divides, or church wounds. Certainly, those relationships may require new boundaries for reconciliation work to rebuild trust; but true repentance works deep healing that is evidenced by changed hearts and lives. When people start apologizing, forgiving, and repenting in visible ways, God is at work beneath the surface. It's a sign dry bones are rattling back to life.

---

4. Neh 8:1–3. The people stood hungry to hear the word after years of exile.

4. Next-Generation Engagement—Not Entertainment but Ownership

When younger believers move from spectators to participants—leading, praying, discipling, dreaming—it's a signal that resurrection life is taking hold. God often signals fresh vision through the emerging generation.

5. Sacrificial Obedience—Even When It Costs Something

New life is evident when people obey God even when it's inconvenient, uncomfortable, or countercultural. When people say yes to hard things—giving, reconciling, serving the poor—it's a sure sign God is breathing again into his church.

These signs don't make headlines. They often show up in small groups, quiet tears, or private obedience. But for the remnant leader who has learned to watch closely, they're like green shoots after a long winter—evidence that God hasn't forgotten, and resurrection power is already at work. Remnant leaders know how to name and nurture new beginnings. They see life on the horizon. They anticipate new birth.

Revival often begins underground. Like a seed sprouting in hidden soil, God's work is frequently invisible before it's undeniable. Jeremiah glimpsed this in a prophetic vision: a branch of an almond tree (Jer 1:11–12). In Hebrew, the word for almond (*shaqed*) sounds like the word for watching (*shoqed*). God was saying prophetically to the people of Judah, "I am watching to see that my word is fulfilled."[5]

Remnant leaders learn to watch with God. To discern faint stirrings of hope. To celebrate small beginnings. To stay present long enough to see the first signs of resurrection. In fact, to go to the tomb in faithful anticipation that one day God will redeem that which appears lifeless.

---

5. Brown, *Jeremiah*, 30–31. Brown explains the Hebrew wordplay as a prophetic pun signifying God's alertness to fulfill his word. Also Thompson, *Book of Jeremiah*, 145–46.

This, for sure, can be challenging. Remaining faithful, even vigilant, in the face of silence and fruitlessness can wreak havoc on a pastor's or leader's mind, heart, and soul. How is one to interpret the silence?

WHEN GOD IS SILENT AND OTHERS PUSH BACK

One of the hardest parts of faithful remnant leadership is the in-between—when God seems quiet and others push back. Jeremiah wrestled deeply with this. In one of his rawest laments, he cries out, "Why is my pain unending and my wound grievous and incurable? You are to me like a deceptive brook, like a spring that fails" (Jer 15:18).

God doesn't scold him for this question. Instead, he offers a holy invitation: "If you repent, I will restore you that you may serve me; if you utter worthy, not worthless, words, you will be my spokesman" (Jer 15:19).

Spiritual silence is not absence. It's formation.

In the silence, God forms steel in our soul. In rejection, he refines our motivations. Remnant leaders must interpret opposition not as a sign of failure but as confirmation that they are standing in a contested space.

Remnant leaders don't pretend they're immune to discouragement—for burnout is a well-greased reality for many. But they return to the presence of God, again and again, when applause fades and their own voice feels weak. That's where the fire is rekindled. It is the call of the remnant leader that bids them to return to the presence of the One who has initiated and defined that call. And in his presence alone there is "fullness of joy" (Ps 16:11). Without it, our flame flickers and we burn out.

PERSONAL RENEWAL WHILE PURSUING REVIVAL

Burnout is not just physical—it's spiritual. Anyone who's been through it knows. And remnant leaders are especially vulnerable when they pour out more than they're being filled.

That's why personal renewal is not a luxury—it's a necessity.

Jesus often withdrew to lonely places to pray (Luke 5:16). Elijah found renewal not in a whirlwind of productivity but in a whisper from God (1 Kgs 19:12). For today's remnant leaders, renewal happens when we stop measuring success by impact and start realigning with intimacy.

Ask yourself, What is fueling me? Am I ministering from overflow—or out of emptiness?

In seasons of waiting, God often invites his leaders to be reawakened internally before the revival happens externally. It starts—and restarts—by remembering our call.

A MODERN THREAD: FAITHFULNESS IN THE SHADOWS

One example of steady, remnant-like faithfulness is John and Vera Mae Perkins, who returned to Mississippi in the 1960s to pursue racial reconciliation and community development. John had every reason not to return—he'd fled the violence and injustice of the Jim Crow South. But God called him back. There, they faced beatings, jailings, and systemic racism. Still, they persevered.

Over the decades, they helped launch ministries, health centers, and leadership programs that have shaped the church's conversation on justice and discipleship for generations.[6] The Perkins' legacy isn't just one of prophetic courage—it's one of long, faithful presence in hard places. It's a legacy of remnant leadership, of enduring obedience.

---

6. Perkins, *Let Justice Roll Down*, for more of their story.

THE SPIRIT IS MOVING, THE REMNANT AWAKES

The faithful remnant doesn't always see the fruit of their labor in their lifetime. They plant, they water, they contend in quiet. And yet, even in seasons of silence or seeming obscurity, the Spirit is moving—resurrecting what once seemed forgotten, repurposing what others abandoned, and forming within leaders a deep-rooted resilience the world cannot manufacture.

The call to stay steady when no one's clapping is not a detour from revival. It's the path. The ones who finish well don't just endure; they embody presence. They keep trusting the whisper, keep tending the flame, and keep showing up in ordinary obedience.

Now, as we come to the end of this journey, we pause—not to wrap things up neatly but to reflect on what God has stirred in us. The final word is not a conclusion.

It's a sending.

An awakening.

A prayer.

My prayer for you—and for me. A prayer for the reviving of the remnant. Will you pray it—and live it—with me?

A REMNANT LEADER'S PRAYER

O God who whispers in the cave and walks among dry bones—awaken us again.

> You have not called us to be impressive, only faithful.
> You have not asked us to go viral but to go deep.
> You do not measure impact in applause but in obedience.
> We yield our need to be seen.
> We surrender our fear of being forgotten.
> We trust that you remember.
> Forge in us a heart that burns without burning out.
> Teach us to tend the slow fire,
> To weep with those no one sees,
> To speak when silence would be safer.

May we raise up leaders, not fans.
May we plant where others see no soil.
May we see the treasure in the one who limps to the back row
Just as we do in the one who takes the stage.
Let our leadership be marked by presence,
Our legacy measured in spiritual grandchildren,
And our days filled with your nearness.
Send us as a remnant—
Not to retreat,
But to rebuild.
Revive the remnant, Lord.
In the name of Jesus,
The Faithful Finisher,
Amen.

REFLECTION AND RENEWAL

Scriptures for Meditation

Jer 15:19-21—God's call to faithful speech and inner restoration.

2 Tim 4:7-8—Paul's charge of finishing the race.

Luke 2:36-38—Anna's quiet prophetic presence.

Jas 5:7-11—The endurance of Job and the call to patience.

Reflection Questions

1. Where do you feel tempted to quit because no one is noticing?
2. How do you discern the difference between God's silence and God's invitation?
3. Who are the faithful finishers around you? How can you honor and learn from them?
4. What signs of hidden life might you be missing in your current setting?

Practice This Week

- Write a letter to a faithful finisher: Identify someone who has stayed the course without applause. Write them a letter of gratitude and encouragement.
- Create a hidden prayer list: Begin a list of quiet prayers and unseen efforts you are making in obedience to God. Revisit it monthly to trace the signs of life God may be birthing through them.

Epilogue
Reviving the Remnant

LONG BEFORE THE MASSES felt the tremors of revival, a remnant prayed.

In the early eighteenth century, the American colonies were spiritually dry—churches were stagnant, nominal Christianity prevailed, and apathy hung like fog over both city and countryside. But in quiet corners—villages, universities, and rural churches—a restless hunger stirred. Jonathan Edwards, a young pastor in Northampton, Massachusetts, witnessed surprising conversions after years of faithful, ordinary preaching. What began as small sparks among his congregation caught fire across New England. The First Great Awakening was born—not because of strategies or spectacle but because a remnant humbled themselves, sought the face of God, and stayed faithful even when little seemed to move.[1]

A few generations later, the Second Great Awakening carried this remnant torch into the next century. It didn't begin in cathedrals or the halls of power but in places like Cane Ridge, Kentucky, where a crowd of frontier Christians—mostly poor, some illiterate, many desperate—gathered to seek God. What followed were massive outdoor revival meetings and a tidal wave of conversions that reshaped American religious life.[2] But again, beneath the platform moments were hidden ones: small prayer meetings, circuit-riding

---

1. Kidd, *Great Awakening*, 95–118.
2. Noll, *America's God*, 170–95.

preachers braving wilderness paths, and lay leaders discipling their neighbors. The awakening spread through firewood conversations, dirt-floor gatherings, and early morning prayers—places where the remnant had prepared the ground.

Throughout history, God has continued this pattern: the Welsh Revival in 1904, the Azusa Street Revival in 1906, the East African Revivals in the mid-twentieth century, the Jesus Movement of the 1970s, the college campus stirrings of the past couple of years, and even today's micro-movements of awakening in Global South house churches and urban renewal hubs in America. These awakenings have differed in form, context, and reach—but almost all of them trace their beginnings to a remnant people crying out for God to do what only he can do.[3]

In every generation, God has moved through the remnant—those willing to live awakened to his presence and committed to his mission. Our generation may be called upon to continue that legacy.

THE AFTERMATH OF CHARLIE KIRK'S ASSASSINATION: A NEW REVIVAL?

As I've reflected on these amazing moments of revival—on how God moved despite opposition, amid suffering, through the faithful few—I find myself wondering whether we are on the threshold of a new awakening. In recent days, America has been shaken by the September 10, 2025, assassination of Charlie Kirk and its ramifications. He was a controversial figure, for sure—politically polarizing, charismatic, decisive in his speech—especially with respect to his Christian faith. Yet, Kirk's death has stirred something: widespread grief, fervent conversations, and for many, it seems, a renewed sense of spiritual longing.

Charlie's widow, Erika Kirk, stood before thousands of worshipers at his memorial and said something breathtaking about her husband's killer: "That young man. That young man on the

---

3. See Orr, *Event of the Century*, for a broad survey, and Lovelace, *Dynamics*, 274–89.

EPILOGUE

cross, our Savior said, 'Father, forgive them for they know not what they do.' That man, that young man, I forgive him. I forgive him, because it was what Christ did, and is what Charlie would do. The answer to hate is not hate."[4]

That moment of forgiveness resonated with something deep—and rare—in public life, calling to mind the Amish community in Nickel Mines, Lancaster County, Pennsylvania, in 2006, who forgave without bitterness after a schoolhouse massacre, and Nelson Mandela, who amid apartheid forgave his captors after twenty-seven years of imprisonment.[5]

Of course, it's far too soon to say whether what's happening now is a genuine awakening—or a grief reaction amplified by polarization. Perhaps both. Time will tell by what endures. What matters most is that faithful people stand in these storm-saturated moments—not for fame, not for political gain, but for one allegiance: the One whose ways are higher, whose heart is mercy, whose love deeply penetrates.

When we live in this kind of love, when we choose forgiveness in the face of hate, when we announce with our words, attitudes, and actions that violence and death and brokenness shall have no victory over us, we echo a remnant tradition that has always borne renewal. "Love never fails," reminds the apostle Paul (1 Cor 13:8). And perhaps here, in love's longevity, we begin to see what lasting awakening might look like.

A REMNANT STARTS WITH A STIRRING

This book has not been about methods of revival per se. It has been about the call of the remnant. It's not been a blueprint but a beckoning—to recover how God renews the church through unlikely leaders and ordinary saints.

Here's a brief retracing of where we've been:

---

4. Danhauer, "Erika Kirk's Emotional Words."
5. Mandela, *Long Walk*, 624–25. Mandela's reflections are humbling.

We uncovered the biblical rhythm of exile, return, and awakening. God doesn't discard the remnants; he rebuilds with them. He whispers in caves and calls forth life from dry bones.

We sat with forgotten figures whose names may not echo in history books but are etched in heaven. They show us that God forms leaders in hidden places.

We explored how suffering and refining are not punishments but sacred invitations to deeper holiness and authority. The remnant is formed in fire.

We learned that the remnant doesn't merely preserve tradition; it reclaims truth with bold humility. Prophets arise, not to shout down culture but to summon it back to the heart of God.

God's renewal begins where human systems fall short—in the margins. The remnant sees treasure in those others overlook.

We also learned that revival that doesn't multiply dies in the pews. The remnant equips, sends, and releases the mission into every neighborhood and nation.

We rediscovered the gospel—not as a formula but as a fire. The remnant tells the story with tears, truth, and testimony.

We examined how resistance doesn't negate the call; it refines it. Remnant leaders don't just survive opposition—they grow through it.

The remnant prepares the way, not just for its own time but for those who come next. Mentorship is a holy handoff. Multiplication is discipleship with foresight.

We saw how remnant leaders breathe life into dry bones, reclaim old spaces, and discover hidden treasures in broken places and overlooked people.

We embraced the quiet strength of faithful finishers. Revival is not built in crowds—it's cultivated in steady hearts.

A remnant starts with a stirring—within the heart of the few, or the one, who are faithful enough to hunger for more of Jesus.

Might that be you?

Appendix

For Pastors—An Eight-Week Sermon Series Starter Outline

SERIES TITLE: REVIVING THE REMNANT

Series Big Idea

When God wants to awaken the world, he starts with the ones no one sees coming.

Week 1: The God Who Shows Up in Burnout

Text: 1 Kgs 19:1–18

Big Idea: God revives the weary not with applause but with presence and purpose.

Teaching Points:

1. Remnants often begin in exhaustion (v. 4)—even prophets hit walls.
2. God's whisper reshapes calling (vv. 11–13)—his voice is often quieter, deeper, and more personal than we expect.
3. A remnant always remains (v. 18)—you are not alone in this wilderness.

APPENDIX

Application: In moments of despair, God speaks identity and sends us back not just restored—but repurposed. Take time this week to listen for God's whisper.

Week 2: Can God Revive Me?

Text: Ezek 37:1–14

Big Idea: God doesn't just revive dry bones—he starts movements from them.

Teaching Points:

1. God leads us to places we want to avoid (v. 1)—the valley isn't failure; it's the setup for glory.
2. Prophesy to what looks dead (v. 4)—faith speaks before flesh appears.
3. The Spirit breathes life into what's been abandoned (v. 10)—revival is a Spirit-powered movement, not a self-help project.

Application: Where do you see "dry bones" in your life or community? Speak God's word over them and trust the Spirit to breathe new life.

Week 3: Awakened to Speak

Text: Jer 1:4–12

Big Idea: God awakens unlikely voices to see and speak what others ignore.

Teaching Points:

1. God often calls the young and insecure (v. 6)—your limitations are God's invitation. [God also calls those who are older and "ready" to hear—Abraham and Sarah, Moses, Anna. The connecting point whether young or older is a readiness to hear and respond in obedient faith.]

2. He touches our mouths before he sends us out (v. 9)—calling comes with God's empowerment.
3. Watch for what God is watching (v. 12, *shaqed/shoqed* wordplay)—awakening begins with attentiveness.

Application: Ask, "What is God watching over to fulfill in your life or your city?" Start there.

Week 4: Holy Disruption

Text: Esth 4:1–17

Big Idea: God places remnant leaders in quiet positions for bold moments.

Teaching Points:

1. Awakening often comes through disruption (v. 3)—grief can lead to holy courage.
2. Even in exile, you're positioned on purpose (v. 14)—"For such a time as this" is not cliché; it's your commission.
3. Courage is choosing faith before certainty (v. 15)—risk is the soil where revival grows.

Application: Where has God positioned you quietly but strategically? Say yes to that hidden assignment this week.

Week 5: Ruined by God's Presence

Text: Isa 6:1–13

Big Idea: Revival begins with a remnant who've been ruined by God's presence.

Teaching Points:

1. Remnant leaders are undone before they're sent (vv. 5–7)—brokenness precedes boldness.

2. God sends Isaiah to a hardened generation (vv. 9–10)—obedience doesn't depend on outcomes.
3. The holy seed is the stump (v. 13)—what looks cut down is actually the starting point.

Application: Where do you feel cut down? Ask God to plant you there with holy seed.

Week 6: The Few Who Changed the World

Text: Acts 1:12—2:4

Big Idea: God ignites movements through small rooms filled with hungry hearts.

Teaching Points:

1. The remnant prays before it proclaims (1:14)—upper rooms precede public revivals.
2. Unity prepares the way for power (2:1)—the Spirit falls where hearts are aligned.
3. Fire marks the remnant's commissioning (2:3–4)—every revival starts with a burning soul.

Application: Are you willing to wait and pray until the fire comes? Make space this week for deeper prayer and listening.

Week 7: The Ones the World Didn't Deserve

Text: Heb 11:32–40

Big Idea: The world overlooks the faithful remnant—but God builds history through them.

Teaching Points:

1. Faithfulness is often forged in obscurity (v. 38)—being unknown doesn't mean being unimportant.

2. Victory and suffering are both part of the story (vv. 33–37)—revival isn't always neat.
3. God completes his work across generations (v. 40)—your faith fuels the future.

Application: Are you willing to run your leg of the race even if no one applauds or cheers? Live this week with eternity in mind.

Week 8: A Remnant for This Moment

Text: Rom 11:1–5

Big Idea: God always has a remnant—and you might be it.

Teaching Points:

1. God's promises are not canceled by human failure (v. 1)—God never wastes a hurt.
2. The remnant is chosen by grace, not popularity (v. 5)—this is about God's mercy, not our merit.
3. Elijah wasn't alone, and neither are you (v. 2–4)—revival may begin in secret but spreads through solidarity.

Application: See yourself as part of God's remnant in this generation. Pray this week, "Lord, awaken your church—and start with me."

Bibliography

Adeney, Miriam. *Kingdom Without Borders: The Untold Story of Global Christianity*. Downers Grove, IL: IVP Academic, 2009.

Aikman, David. *Jesus in Beijing: How Christianity Is Transforming China and Changing the Global Balance of Power*. Washington, DC: Regnery, 2003.

Alpha USA. "What Is Alpha?" https://alphausa.org/about.

Augustine. *Confessions*. Translated by Henry Chadwick. Oxford: Oxford University Press, 1991.

Barna, George. "CRC's Barna Describes Faith and Cultural Trends Likely to Emerge in 2025." GeorgeBarna.com, Jan. 15, 2025. https://georgebarna.com/2025/01/2025-trends-outlook/.

Bauer, Walter, et al. *Greek-English Lexicon of the New Testament and Other Early Christian Literature*. 2nd ed. Chicago: University of Chicago Press, 1979.

Beck, Michael. *Deep Roots, Wild Branches*. Franklin, TN: Seedbed, 2019.

Block, Daniel I. *The Book of Ezekiel, Chapters 25–48*. New International Commentary on the Old Testament. Grand Rapids: Eerdmans, 1998.

Breen, Mike. *Building a Discipling Culture: How to Release a Missional Movement by Discipling People Like Jesus Did*. Pawleys Island, SC: 3DM Ministries, 2011.

Brother Lawrence. *The Practice of the Presence of God*. Translated by John J. Delaney. Garden City, NY: Image, 1977.

Brown, Michael. *Jeremiah: A Commentary Based on Jeremiah in the New International Version*. Grand Rapids: Baker Academic, 2010.

Brueggemann, Walter. *Hopeful Imagination: Prophetic Voices in Exile*. Minneapolis: Fortress, 1986.

Chilcote, Paul Wesley. *Recapturing the Wesleys' Vision: An Introduction to the Faith of John and Charles Wesley*. Downers Grove, IL: IVP Academic, 2004.

Childress, Jesse. "Engaging Relational Evangelism in the Back-to-School Season." Summit Ministries, Aug. 3, 2023. https://www.summit.org/resources/articles/engaging-relational-evangelism-in-the-back-to-school-season/.

Christian Endeavor. "About Christian Endeavor." https://www.ceworks.faith/about.

BIBLIOGRAPHY

Church in Chains. "Vietnam." Feb. 17, 2025. https://www.churchinchains.ie/country-profiles/vietnam/.

Church Multiplication Coalition. *International Manual, 2017–2018 Edition.* https://www.4cmcinternational.org/wp-content/uploads/2018/11/CMC-Manual-2017-.pdf.

Claiborne, Shane. *The Irresistible Revolution: Living as an Ordinary Radical.* Grand Rapids: Zondervan, 2006.

Clinton, Catherine. *Harriet Tubman: The Road to Freedom.* New York: Little, Brown, 2004.

Crisp, Regan. "Bell Tower Coffee: Portland's Serene Church Cafe." Sprudge, Feb. 29, 2016. https://sprudge.com/bell-tower-coffee-94464.html.

Dallimore, Arnold A. *Susannah Wesley: The Mother of John and Charles Wesley.* Chicago: Moody, 1993.

Danhauer, Whitney. "Erika Kirk's Emotional Words Inspired Tim Allen to Make a Life-Changing Decision." *Parade*, Aug. 16, 2025. https://parade.com/news/tim-allen-erika-kirk-inspiration.

Drummond, Lewis. *Spurgeon: Prince of Preachers.* Grand Rapids: Kregel, 1992.

Elliott, Debbie, et al. "10 Years After the Deadly Church Shooting, a New History of 'Mother Emanuel.'" NPR, June 14, 2025. https://www.npr.org/2025/06/14/nx-s1-5391851/kevin-sack-mother-emanuel.

Eskridge, Larry. *God's Forever Family: The Jesus People Movement in America.* Oxford: Oxford University Press, 2013.

Evans, Eifion. *The Welsh Revival of 1904.* Bridgend, Wales: Bryntirion, 1969.

Ford, Lance, et al. *The Starfish and the Spirit: Unleashing the Leadership Potential of Churches and Organizations.* Grand Rapids: Zondervan, 2021.

Frost, Michael. *The Road to Missional: Journey to the Center of the Church.* Grand Rapids: Baker, 2011.

Fujimura, Makoto. *Art and Faith: A Theology of Making.* New Haven: Yale University Press, 2020.

Giglio, Louie. *The Comeback: It's Not Too Late and You're Never Too Far.* Nashville: Nelson, 2015.

Green, Michael. *Evangelism in the Early Church.* Grand Rapids: Eerdmans, 2003.

Hardwick, Lamar. *Disability and the Church: A Vision for Diversity and Inclusion.* Downers Grove, IL: IVP, 2021.

Hattaway, Paul. *The Heavenly Man.* Oxford: Monarch, 2002.

Hawes, Jennifer Berry. *Grace Will Lead Us Home: The Charleston Church Massacre and the Hard, Inspiring Journey to Forgiveness.* New York: St. Martin's, 2019.

Heffernan, Thomas J., ed. and trans. *The Passion of Perpetua and Felicity.* Oxford: Oxford University Press, 2012.

Hirsch, Alan. *The Forgotten Ways: Reactivating the Missional Church.* Grand Rapids: Brazos, 2006.

Hirsch, Alan, and Michael Frost. *The Shaping of Things to Come: Innovation and Mission for the 21st-Century Church.* Grand Rapids: Baker, 2003.

Hirsch, Alan, and Tim Catchim. *The Permanent Revolution: Apostolic Imagination and Practice for the 21st-Century Church.* San Francisco: Jossey-Bass, 2012.

Im, Daniel. *You Are What You Do: And Six Other Lies About Work, Life, and Love.* Nashville: B&H, 2020.

International Project. "Philosophy of Ministry." https://internationalproject.org/philosophy-of-ministry/.

Kidd, Thomas S. *The Great Awakening: The Roots of Evangelical Christianity in Colonial America.* New Haven: Yale University Press, 2007.

Kolodiejchuk, Brian, ed. *Mother Teresa: Come Be My Light—The Private Writings of the Saint of Calcutta.* New York: Doubleday, 2007.

Liardon, Robert. *God's Generals: The Revivalists.* New Kensington, PA: Whitaker House, 1996.

Lovelace, Richard. *Dynamics of Spiritual Life: An Evangelical Theology of Renewal.* Downers Grove, IL: IVP Academic, 1979.

Mandela, Nelson. *Long Walk to Freedom.* Boston: Little, Brown, 1994.

Mandryk, Jason. *Operation World: The Definitive Prayer Guide to Every Nation.* Downers Grove, IL: IVP, 2010.

Monbiot, George. *Feral: Rewilding the Land, the Sea, and Human Life.* Chicago: University of Chicago Press, 2014.

Mounce, William D. *Basics of Biblical Greek Grammar.* 3rd ed. Grand Rapids: Zondervan, 2009.

Mulinde, John, and Mark Daniel. *Prayer Altars: A Strategy That Is Changing Nations.* Orlando, FL: World Trumpet, 2011.

Noll, Mark A. *America's God: From Jonathan Edwards to Abraham Lincoln.* Oxford: Oxford University Press, 2002.

Nouwen, Henri J. M. *The Wounded Healer: Ministry in Contemporary Society.* New York: Doubleday, 1972.

Orr, J. Edwin. *The Event of the Century: The 1904–1905 Welsh Revival.* Oxford: Christian Literature Crusade, 1989.

Palau, Andrew. *The Secret Life of a Fool: One Man's Raw Journey from Shame to Grace.* Colorado Springs, CO: Worthy, 2012.

Perkins, John. *Let Justice Roll Down: John Perkins Tells His Own Story.* Ventura, CA: Regal, 1976.

Peterson, Eugene H. *A Long Obedience in the Same Direction: Discipleship in an Instant Society.* Downers Grove, IL: InterVarsity, 1980.

Pullinger, Jackie. *Chasing the Dragon.* Minneapolis: Chosen, 2006.

Qureshi, Nabeel. *Seeking Allah, Finding Jesus.* Grand Rapids: Zondervan, 2014.

Raboteau, Albert J. *Slave Religion: The "Invisible Institution" in the Antebellum South.* Oxford: Oxford University Press, 2004.

Rohr, Richard. *Everything Belongs: The Gift of Contemplative Prayer.* New York: Crossroad, 2003.

Rosenberg, Joel C. *Inside the Revival: How God Is Moving in the Middle East.* Carol Stream, IL: Tyndale, 2022.

Scandrette, Mark. *Practicing the Way of Jesus: Life Together in the Kingdom of Love*. Downers Grove, IL: IVP, 2011.
Tari, Mel. *Like a Mighty Wind*. Plainfield, NJ: Logos International, 1971.
Ten Boom, Corrie. *The Hiding Place*. New York: Bantam, 1971.
Thompson, John A. *The Book of Jeremiah*. New International Commentary on the Old Testament. Grand Rapids: Eerdmans, 1980.
Wallace, Charles. *Susanna Wesley: The Complete Writings*. Oxford: Oxford University Press, 1997.
Wiersbe, Warren W. *50 People Every Christian Should Know: Learning from Spiritual Giants of the Faith*. Grand Rapids: Baker, 2009.
Willard, Dallas. *The Divine Conspiracy: Rediscovering Our Hidden Life in God*. San Francisco: HarperOne, 1998.
Woolverton, David E. *Mission Rift: Leading Through Church Conflict*. Minneapolis: Fortress, 2021.
———. *Prophet and Loss: Embracing Grief, Nurturing Resilience, and Harnessing Authentic Leadership*. Eugene, OR: Wipf & Stock, 2024.
Wurmbrand, Richard. *Tortured for Christ*. Bartlesville, OK: Voice of the Martyrs, 2013.

www.ingramcontent.com/pod-product-compliance
Lightning Source LLC
Chambersburg PA
CBHW051106160426
43193CB00010B/1335